THE
LADY
AND THE
OCTOPUS

How JEANNE VILLEPREUX-POWER
Invented Aquariums
and Revolutionized Marine Biology

DANNA STAAF

CAROLRHODA BOOKS

Minneapolis

To Dad, my first partner in aquariophily

Carolrhoda Books®
An imprint of Lerner Publishing Group, Inc.
241 First Avenue North
Minneapolis, MN 55401 USA

For reading levels and more information, look up this title at www.lernerbooks.com.

Maps and diagram on pages 14, 24, 76, and 112 by Laura K. Westlund.

Designed by Danielle Carnito.
Main body text set in Bembo Std.
Typeface provided by Monotype Typography.

Library of Congress Cataloging-in-Publication Data

Names: Staaf, Danna, author.
Title: The lady and the octopus : how Jeanne Villepreux-Power invented aquariums and revolutionized marine biology / Danna Staaf.
Description: Minneapolis : Carolrhoda Books, [2022] | Includes bibliographical references and index. | Audience: Ages 10–18 | Audience: Grades 7–9 | Summary: "Follow the remarkable journey of Jeanne Villepreux-Power from her childhood in a small French village to her life as a naturalist in nineteenth-century Messina, Sicily, where she conducted groundbreaking research and invented aquariums" —Provided by publisher.
Identifiers: LCCN 2021051154 (print) | LCCN 2021051155 (ebook) | ISBN 9781728415772 (library binding) | ISBN 9781728460833 (ebook)
Subjects: LCSH: Villepreux-Power, Jeanne, 1794–1871—Juvenile literature. | Women marine biologists—France—Biography—Juvenile literature. | Women naturalists—France—Biography—Juvenile literature.
Classification: LCC QH31.V48 S73 2022 (print) | LCC QH31.V48 (ebook) | DDC 578.77092 [B]—dc23/eng/20211104

LC record available at https://lccn.loc.gov/2021051154
LC ebook record available at https://lccn.loc.gov/2021051155

Manufactured in the United States of America
1-48735-49145-5/2/2022

CONTENTS

INTRODUCTION • 4
THE MYSTERY OF THE ARGONAUTS

CHAPTER ONE • 10
THE SEAMSTRESS

CHAPTER TWO • 23
THE EXPLORER

CHAPTER THREE • 41
THE INVENTOR

CHAPTER FOUR • 58
THE DETECTIVE

CHAPTER FIVE • 78
THE REPORTER

CHAPTER SIX • 94
THE LUMINARY

EPILOGUE • 110
MARINE BIOLOGY TODAY AND TOMORROW

Author's Note • 116

Timeline • 118

Glossary • 123

Source Notes • 125

Bibliography • 129

Further Reading • 133

Index • 134

THE
MYSTERY
OF THE
ARGONAUTS

Sleeves rolled up, arms dripping seawater, Jeanne Villepreux-Power holds the most beautiful seashell she's ever seen—and tries to break it. The translucent pearly material flexes under her fingers. Several long arms reach out of the shell and wrap their suckered lengths around Jeanne's hands. She adjusts her grip, not wanting to hurt the octopus who lives inside. She tries a new angle, applying more pressure, until finally—*crack!* A large piece of shell comes off in her hand, leaving a jagged gap in the once-perfect spiral.

Jeanne leans over the side of her boat to put the broken shell and octopus back into an underwater wooden enclosure that she designed. The sky and the Mediterranean Sea are both clear and warm, and Jeanne settles in to watch the octopus with the broken shell. She takes notes and sketches as her small craft bobs gently in the waves just off the Italian island of Sicily, surrounded by the cries of seagulls and fishermen. It is 1833, and she is a working scientist, trying to solve an ancient puzzle. The octopus, too, is hard at work. She is fixing her shell.

Of course, octopuses are famously squishy—they have no bones, no teeth, no scales, and usually no shells. Their only hard part is the beak they use to eat. As long as that beak can fit through a crack or under a rock, the rest of the octopus's body can squeeze along with it.

But this kind of octopus is different. She is called an argonaut, and she lives in a delicate coiled shell. For thousands of years, people have wondered how the argonaut gets her shell. Does she steal it like a hermit crab or grow it like a snail? Jeanne intends to find out.

Scientists before Jeanne have guessed and argued about the answer to this question, based on their studies of dead argonauts. But Jeanne wants to study these animals while they are still alive. Such an undertaking is not as easy as bringing a live tortoise or weasel-like pine marten into her house (which Jeanne has also done). Octopuses are aquatic, so Jeanne has had to design special underwater homes to keep them alive while she observes them. She began with glass aquariums and then developed wooden cages that could be anchored to the seafloor. Nothing like this existed before. There are no public aquariums, no fish tanks in doctors' waiting rooms. (In 1833 doctors all make house calls, anyway.)

Learning to pronounce names from languages not our own can take some effort, but it's an important way to show respect to people both living and dead. After all, none of us like to hear our name mispronounced!

Jeanne Villepreux-Power sounds close to ZHEN VEEL-prooh POW-er. You can hear it spoken by French historian Josquin Debaz at https://www.dannastaaf.com /p/the-lady-and-octopus.html.

A young female argonaut floats near the water's surface, clinging to the inside of her shell with the suckers on her arms.

As Jeanne watches the octopus mending her shell, she might feel a twinge of sympathy. Like the octopus,

Jeanne has done her fair share of mending, and like the octopus, she has labored to create something eye-catchingly beautiful. Seventeen years ago, when she was a young dressmaker in Paris, France, Jeanne sewed a wedding gown for a princess. Though it had nothing to do with the sea, that remarkable feat set her on the path that led her here. Because of the gown, she married a merchant; because of the merchant, she moved to Sicily; and because of Sicily, she met the argonaut. Now she's up to her elbows in seawater, rather than fabric, and her attention has shifted from chemises to shells.

For most kinds of octopuses, distinguishing females from males is difficult. Both sexes have eight arms attached directly to their head, which bears two large eyes and a siphon for breathing and jetting. A large soft body called a mantle contains their organs—gills, stomach, kidneys, and three separate hearts. The mantle's size and shape are similar in both sexes. The only difference is that one of the adult male's arms is slightly modified to deliver sperm, with a groove along its length and a rounded tip.

The giant Pacific octopus, a relative of the argonauts Jeanne studied, is often displayed in public aquariums.

ON HISTORICAL ACCURACY

A biography presents the facts of a person's life: places and dates, experiences and discoveries. It offers historical context: the political and cultural movements a person lived through. Ideally, it tells a human story.

To get it all right, biographers conduct research. We read what the subjects of our biographies wrote and what has already been written about them. We hunt for drawings, photographs, and movies of them. Unfortunately, Jeanne lived and died before the invention of audio or video recordings, and even photography became available only late in her life.

Jeanne wrote volumes and extensively illustrated her work, but most of her notes and drawings were destroyed in a shipwreck. This biography relies heavily on her surviving books and papers, as well as a handful of articles written about her during her lifetime.

We can imagine aspects of Jeanne's life based on how women of her age, race, wealth, and social status typically lived in the various places she called home. We can also make inferences by combining different sources of information. For example, if we know that a famous naturalist visited Sicily while Jeanne was there, we can guess that the two of them met and conversed. And if they were both interested in reptiles, then what do you suppose they talked about?

We do know that Jeanne would not have described herself as a scientist. That word didn't even exist until 1834, and then it took a while to enter common usage. I've chosen to call Jeanne and her colleagues scientists anyway, because that's how we think of them today.

In this book, you'll come across plenty of "maybes" and "probablys" to qualify educated guesses about Jeanne's life. You'll also read direct

Jeanne Villepreux-Power lived through the invention and popularization of photography. This portrait was taken by the famous French photographer André-Adolphe-Eugène Disdéri.

quotes from Jeanne and her friends, telling as much of the story as possible in their own words.

Perhaps more historical sources will one day come to light—literally dredged from the deep, if the shipwreck is ever salvaged. They would doubtless improve our understanding of Jeanne and her work, and might even contradict some of my educated guesses. I like to think that Jeanne would be understanding of such errors. After all, she was wrong about a few things in the course of her research, but she did her best with what was available to her. That is what I, too, have done.

But again, this octopus is different. At the time Jeanne begins her work, scientists know only about female argonauts, who use their shells to brood their eggs. No one has ever seen a male argonaut. Perhaps, as a few people think, males don't exist. But Jeanne wonders. Sometimes little wormlike creatures are found inside female argonauts, and although other scientists call them parasites, Jeanne thinks they may be the males of the species.

Jeanne is full of ideas, as well as the patience, dedication, and resources to explore them. That's why she's sitting wet-armed in a boat in the port of Messina, instead of staying home to manage her household as well-off women of her time are expected to do.

Although European society in 1833 is depressingly sexist, Jeanne is both white and wealthy, a privileged position from which she will convince many of her male colleagues to recognize her accomplishments. Despite laws that prohibit women from voting in an election or attending a university, she'll become the first female member of the local scientific organization, the Gioenia Academy, and will join many other learned societies during her life. When an "aquarium craze" sweeps across Europe and the United States, a widely respected fellow scientist will support her efforts to be credited as the inventor of aquariums.

The city of Messina, Sicily, and its surroundings became Jeanne's home and laboratory. This panorama by Italian painter Carlo Bossoli depicts Messina in 1858, later in Jeanne's life.

But she'll be no stranger to disappointment. A man whom she entrusts with her report on argonaut biology will steal her ideas and present them as his own. A ship that she entrusts with sixteen cases of invaluable specimens, drawings, and notes will sink en route from Sicily to England.

Partly because of this tragedy, which destroys so much of her scientific legacy, in the years after her death Jeanne will be often forgotten. Her story will also be revived from time to time, although storytellers will sometimes alter the facts and add their own embellishments to make the story more romantic.

Today, through the efforts of historians, scientists, artists, and writers around the world, Jeanne is finding her place in history as a trailblazing inventor and scientist. At a time when studying marine biology usually meant looking at dead fish on a table, Jeanne insisted on observing live animals, as often as possible in their natural habitats. While other biologists presented their conjectures and hypotheses as facts, Jeanne was a determined designer of experiments as well as aquariums. Experiments *test* hypotheses, and experimentation is a cornerstone of modern science. Jeanne's revolutionary approach yielded results, which she shared widely by writing in multiple languages and doggedly responding to criticism. It is through Jeanne's own work that we know her best, and none of her research was dearer to her than her studies on that strange and beautiful octopus, the argonaut.

CHAPTER ONE

THE
SEAMSTRESS

*The mollusk when born, is naked and incomplete . . . it becomes
progressively developed in the end of the spire of the parent argonaut;
and after a given time it goes on forming its shell.*

— JEANNE VILLEPREUX-POWER, 1839

The girl who would grow up to reinvent marine biology never saw the sea as a child. She was raised in Juillac, France, about 200 kilometers (124 miles) from the closest ocean—and more than 400 kilometers (250 miles) south of Paris. Today a car could make those trips in a matter of hours, but in 1794, when Jeanne was born, horses were the fastest method of transportation. Riding to the sea or to the capital would have taken days.

Juillac was a remote country town, and a good thing too for Jeanne's family.

WELCOME TO REVOLUTIONARY FRANCE

In the 1790s the French Revolution was in full swing, with Paris as its violent epicenter. The inspiring ideals of *Liberty, Equality, Brotherhood* were offset by mass beheadings, drownings, widespread vandalism, and theft. What began as an uprising of commoners against the monarchy and clergy turned into a dictatorship of the so-called French First Republic. A broad interpretation of "equality" led to dangerous laws, such as one that let any person claim to be a doctor and treat patients. The guillotine was invented to execute traitors efficiently, and the new government interpreted "traitor" even more broadly than "equality."

But that was all distant news in Juillac, where townsfolk busy with their daily lives probably cared less about political executions in Paris than about local marriages, births, and deaths. The year that the guillotine fell on King Louis XVI, 1793, also saw the wedding of Jeanne's parents: Pierre Villepreux, a Juillac police officer, and Jeanne Nicot from Limoges, a town just a couple of days' walk to the north. The young couple was well educated, both having learned to read and write at a time when most French women and about half of French men were illiterate.

The community of Juillac nestles in the hills of central France. Its population was recorded as 2,126 in 1793, the year that Jeanne's parents were married.

They were also reasonably well off, with a dowry (money paid to the groom by the parents of the bride) from the Nicot family.

Here's the domestic news for the next year, 1794: Madame Jeanne Villepreux was pregnant. Here's the national news: the Revolution had become the Reign of Terror. The radical Maximilien Robespierre and his fellows were executing anyone sympathetic to the monarchy, anyone sympathetic to the Catholic Church, and anyone who didn't fall into either category but happened to be in the wrong place at the wrong time. (The revolutionaries also abolished slavery in all French colonies. It had been abolished in France itself 479 years earlier by King Louis X, with the idealistic declaration "France signifies freedom."

When Jeanne was born, France was reeling from the bloody aftermath of King Louis XVI's execution in 1793. This period in history continued to fascinate people long after it took place; this wood engraving was published in 1900.

By contrast, colonial abolition was primarily motivated by revolts of the enslaved populations.) The Terror ended in July when Robespierre was guillotined, and in September the Villepreux parents welcomed their first child: a daughter.

Although we now record her birthday as September 25, 1794, at the time her family was required to call it the 4th of Vendémiaire, Year 3 of the Republican calendar. The revolutionaries had cleverly devised this new timekeeping method to avoid all references to royalty or religion. It followed an efficient, logical decimal system, including ten-day weeks and ten-hour days.

In fact, the Republic's lofty ambition was to reinvent *everything* with efficiency and logic. While some efforts flopped (the new calendar was abandoned after twelve years), the metric system became an international standard for measurement. The reverence for rationality that characterized revolutionary France contributed to a broader European shift toward systematic logic. Jeanne would later bring this approach to her scientific pursuits, helping to ground the field of marine biology in experiment and evidence rather than armchair theorizing.

BIRTH OF THE METRIC SYSTEM

If you grew up in the United States, you're probably used to measuring temperature in Fahrenheit, distance in miles, height in feet, and weight in pounds—a set of measurements known as the US customary system. If you grew up almost anywhere else in the world, then you use Celsius, kilometers, meters, and kilograms. These measurements belong to the metric system, which owes its existence to the French Revolution.

US customary units, and the closely related British imperial units, are both derived from English units that had been around for hundreds of years. This older system has several flaws. You have to memorize a large set of arbitrary numbers in order to understand it: 12 inches make a foot, 16 ounces a pound, 5,280 feet a mile. Water freezes at 32°F and boils at 212°F. What's more, for most of history there was no universal standard for these units, so what you really meant by a foot or a pound depended on where you lived and who you had to agree with.

A decimal system, which uses multiples of ten to convert between units, is a welcome simplification. So 100 centimeters make a meter, 1,000 meters a kilometer, and 1,000 grams a kilogram. Water freezes at 0°C and boils at 100°C. This astonishingly organized system was born in the chaos of the French Revolution, when an international group of scientists convened in Paris and created precise standards for each unit. The French Republic officially adopted this new metric system on April 7, 1795 (though as you may have guessed, they would have given it a different name—specifically 18 Germinal, Year 2).

The six-month-old Jeanne undoubtedly did not care whether she drank milk in ounces or milliliters, nor whether she crawled across the floor in feet or meters. (To be historically precise, while prerevolutionary France did use *pieds*, or feet, that country's equivalent of the English fluid ounce was the *roquille*.) Nevertheless, the adoption of the metric system in her home country was an auspicious start for the baby scientist. Now researchers all around the world could record and compare results in a consistent, reliable way. Even American scientists have embraced the metric system in their work, although they may still glance out the window and think automatically in Fahrenheit, "Looks like it might hit 80 today."

Not just American scientists but also government employees and many industry workers throughout the country regularly use metric measurements. So why does the United States still seem to be so stuck on imperial units? Well, it's a big country with a lot of road signs in miles, a lot of thermometers in Fahrenheit, and a lot of people who know their own height only in feet and inches. "Metrication" *is* happening; it's just extremely slow. In 1975 the Metric Conversion Act declared metric "the preferred system," but it wasn't until 1991 that the executive branch of the government switched over. Today, food labels are required to provide metric measurements, over-the-counter drugs and prescription medications have metric dosage, and the game of Ultimate Frisbee uses discs made to metric standards.

Here's a thoughtful prediction from math professor Russ Rowlett: "The American economy of the 22nd century may be completely metric, but probably Americans will still call 30 centimeters a 'foot' and 1,600 meters a 'mile.'"

GROWING UP WITH SHOES AND SHEEP

As the first Villepreux child, Jeanne was named after her mother, but her family called her by the nickname Lili. Although the Terror was over and the guillotine retired, the years of Jeanne's childhood boiled with national and international strife. In Paris, food and fuel were scarce, and uprising followed uprising. And from 1796 to 1815, Napoleon Bonaparte led the French army in wars against Great Britain, Austria, Italy, and half a dozen other nations.

Meanwhile, in the relatively quiet French countryside, Jeanne learned to read and write—probably taught by her mother, as elementary schools were uncommon—and helped care for two little sisters and a brother. Her mother, who before marriage had lived with an uncle who was a master tailor, probably taught Jeanne to sew and

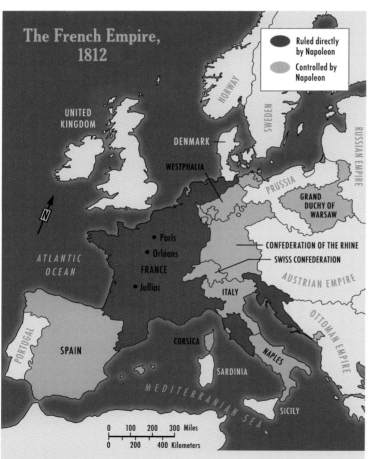

embroider as well. Her father left his job as a police officer for a stint in road-building; then he switched again to shoemaking. In the early 1800s, when walking was the only way for most people to get anywhere, building roads and making shoes were two sides of the same coin. With a solid road and a sturdy pair of shoes, you could see the world with your own two feet. Did this realization dawn on Jeanne as she watched her father work? Did she feel a stirring toward adventure, this girl who would grow into a multilingual traveler with homes in three countries?

As the eldest child, she may have lent a hand in the family business and picked up practical skills in so doing—cutting,

While Jeanne was growing up, the French Empire was growing too, until Napoleon controlled most of western Europe. Not pictured are the many French-occupied colonies in Asia, Africa, and the Americas.

shaping, and stitching leather. Like most rural folk, the Villepreux family also kept livestock, so Jeanne learned to mind sheep, cattle, pigs, and chickens. Her later writing would reveal a fascination with nature and a total lack of squeamishness, suggesting that as a child she likely reveled in this barnyard company.

When Jeanne was ten years old, she became a citizen of an empire instead of a republic. Napoleon Bonaparte had crowned himself emperor of the French. This development probably didn't change her life much, especially not in comparison with the family tragedy that occurred the same year— the death of Jeanne's five-year-old sister, Gabrielle. With limited sanitation and medical care, such losses were all too common. Gabrielle might have died of diarrhea, an infected cut, the flu, or any of a number of other maladies. Jeanne, who had helped care for her sister since infancy, must have been heartbroken.

No doubt distracted by grief, their father Pierre mistakenly told the recordkeeper that his five-year-old

An extremely capable military leader and politician, Napoleon Bonaparte took advantage of the chaos and fear left in the wake of the French Revolution to rig his own "election" as emperor of the French. His coronation took place on December 2, 1804; he was painted by François Gérard the following year.

daughter *Jeanne* had died, creating an official confusion that would follow the real Jeanne the rest of her life. (Remember, Jeanne had always been called Lili. Pierre may well have forgotten which of his daughters had the legal name Jeanne.)

We can only imagine what a blow it was to the family when Jeanne's mother died the very next year. As with Gabrielle's death, the cause isn't recorded, but in a small village without a hospital, there were all too many possibilities. Jeanne was not quite twelve years old.

Her father soon remarried. He'd found enough success with roads and shoes that he became a merchant—a buyer and seller of goods, rather than a mere craftsman. His new wife, at twenty-three years old, was closer in age to Jeanne than to her forty-six-year-old husband. We don't know whether Jeanne's young stepmother was a source of comfort and support as she grieved the loss of her sister and mother or whether Jeanne felt resentful of the new family situation. She was probably expected to care not just for her surviving sister and brother but also for the half brother that soon arrived. She remained the only literate child in a house that contained few books and even fewer spare hours to read them.

Regardless of how amiable or awkward her family relationships were, Jeanne was an inquisitive, educated teenager eager to explore beyond her childhood home. Several romanticized early biographies claim that Jeanne found a job as a shepherdess for another family, but later biographers point out that most families in the country had their own children to tend their livestock. If Jeanne herded sheep, they were probably the Villepreux sheep. Without citing sources, the same early biographies suggest that the son of her supposed employer fell in love with Jeanne, and his family didn't approve. Jeanne never wrote of such an experience, but lovesick or not, she may have felt restless in the country.

As an adult, Jeanne would display an endless enthusiasm for discovery and exploration. At the age of seventeen, it seems likely that she aspired to find her own way in the world. Although history doesn't record the details, she arranged for a job in Paris, perhaps as a kitchen maid. Now all she had to do was get there.

JEANNE ON HER OWN

It was 1812, and war between France and the rest of Europe had dragged on as long as Jeanne could remember. While Napoleon marched his great army deeper into Russia, Jeanne faced a journey that must have seemed nearly as daunting—450 kilometers (280 miles) to Paris, all on foot.

She set off on the sixteen-day trek with a cousin who was bringing a herd of cows to the Paris slaughterhouses. We don't know his name or age, or how well he and Jeanne were acquainted before they became traveling companions. Unfortunately, it might have been better for Jeanne to have traveled alone. More than halfway to Paris, near the city of Orléans, the cousin she had trusted as a guardian assaulted her.

Jeanne fled into the city. There's no evidence that her cousin was ever detained by police; most likely, he continued on his journey. But Jeanne, still technically a minor, ended up a ward of the local authorities. The Orléans magistrate obstructed her further travel with demands for identifying paperwork and a monetary deposit. What monstrous unfairness, to require the victim of an attack to prove herself before releasing her from custody!

Jeanne handed over the money and then wrote to the mayor of Juillac pleading for his support. Her handwriting in the letter is visibly uneven, with minimal punctuation and no capitals. She had spent more time caring for siblings and livestock, no doubt, than practicing cursive. But she was determined to make her case.

a letter that you will receive from the magistrate of security informs you that I am in this city without being able to leave to go to paris where I have employment if you do not certify that my father consents to this trip. you know what my position was, and the reasons for my departure. please have I beg you the kindness to send me a favorable certificate addressed to this magistrate who demanded a deposit that I have given I think my father will not contradict you. by extending this service of your justice allow me to assure you of my most perfect consideration with which I am mister your very humble servant lili villepreux

While she waited for his reply, Jeanne stayed in a convent in Orléans. This city is forever associated with Jeanne d'Arc, more commonly known in English as Joan of Arc, the "maid of Orléans" whose courage and skill delivered it from siege in 1429. The memory of such a powerful young woman, who had defied all expectations and followed her own path, may have been a source of solace and inspiration to Jeanne—who shared her name and was also, at seventeen, the same age Joan had been when she saved the city.

Joan of Arc (Jeanne d'Arc in French) fought to defend France from invading English troops in the Hundred Years' War. Later captured and put on trial in England, she testified that she had been inspired by visions of saints and was burned at the stake for heresy.

A convent at the time was not only the home of nuns but also a community center organized and staffed by these women. It often served as an orphanage, a homeless shelter, a hospital, and a school. During the French Revolution, religious life had been outlawed and many nuns had been killed or forced to marry, but many others survived in hiding and reopened their convents when Napoleon came to power. Jeanne was probably not the only young woman living in the quiet company of the Orléans nuns, waiting for the next step in her life's journey. Perhaps she used the time to practice her artistic skills. Although no drawings or embroidery survive from Jeanne's youth, the talent evident in her later work suggests a history of practice. At last, the papers arrived from Juillac. She set off for the final few days of her trip.

At the end of 1812, Jeanne's tired feet brought her to the streets of Paris. Paris! It was a city in transition, still in disarray from the Revolution but being rebuilt by Napoleon to rival the glory of ancient Rome. The church bells, which had been silenced during the Revolution, rang once more. Although the Eiffel Tower wouldn't show up for another seventy years, the Arc de Triomphe was under construction, and the Louvre, renamed Musée Napoléon, had opened to display thousands of artistic masterpieces (most of them filched from other countries during Napoleon's military campaigns).

Unfortunately, whatever job Jeanne had thought would be waiting for her in Paris wasn't waiting anymore. What was she to do?

A young working-class woman arriving in a big city had several options, though they weren't all pleasant. She might become a servant to the wealthy— not an easy life and not one with much opportunity for advancement. She might become a prostitute, a profession that was both common and legal. Prostitutes who serviced the rich could live quite comfortable lives, while those with less wealthy clients often struggled to support themselves and the children they bore—and all of them risked contracting sexually transmitted infections, such as syphilis. Jeanne's story might easily have ended in obscurity or tragedy.

But Paris offered other opportunities too, and Jeanne had a remarkable mix of good fortune, determination, and spirit. She could read and write, for one thing, and sew and embroider, for another. She was also graced with the confidence of an eldest child who had been looking after herself and others for a third of her life. In short order, she found work as an assistant to a milliner who made hats for the Paris elite.

REVOLUTIONARY FRENCH FASHION

Paris has been a pinnacle of European fashion for centuries, ever since the 1600s when King Louis XIV decided he had to have the most, the biggest, and the prettiest of everything. The style of the French court got more elaborate with every passing year, until royals found themselves decked out in gigantic wigs, buried under layers of bows and embroidery.

The absurdly expensive dress of aristocrats was part of the fuel for the French Revolution. Ordinary people were starving in the streets while the nobility added ever more gold to their gowns. Queen Marie Antoinette wore such enormous dresses it's hard to imagine how she could even move, let alone sit down or eat a meal.

Then she decided to show off a radical *new* fashion, which further infuriated the French citizenry. At the time of the Revolution, enthusiasm for the simpler styles of ancient Greece and Rome had already been growing throughout Europe. Dresses were becoming lighter and more natural-looking as women abandoned uncomfortable corsets for high empire waists. However, these light dresses, or chemises, were hardly formal wear—until Marie Antoinette posed for a portrait in one.

Just like plenty of folks today, people in the 1800s were obsessed with following the fashion choices of the rich and famous. If Instagram had been available, they'd have been all over it. Marie Antoinette's dress was dubbed the *chemise à la reine*, a chemise in the queen's style, and it galled the

Marie Antoinette en chemise, the controversial 1783 portrait of the queen

public just as much as her gold-encrusted finery had done. It was a caricature of rural clothing, something worn by a queen who wanted to pretend to be a shepherdess without ever having touched a real sheep, let alone stepped in sheep dung.

Marie Antoinette was guillotined in 1793 for her fashion crimes (among other reasons). Jeanne was born the next year.

By the time Jeanne arrived in Paris and began her work as a seamstress, the ornate styles of the old monarchy had been fully swept aside in favor of airy, classical dresses. Did Jeanne hear about the scandal of the *chemise à la reine* from her employer? As an actual shepherdess, would she have laughed at the idea of a queen trying to imitate her hardworking lifestyle simply by donning a lightweight dress? And yet, Jeanne would go on to create a fashion descendant of Marie Antoinette's chemise when she was hired to design the dress for a Sicilian princess's wedding.

The princess's gown had an empire waist, a low neckline, and puffy sleeves, like everyday dresses of the time. But it was intricately decorated, from the layers of lace around the collar to the densely embroidered skirt to the train of heavy brocade. It's such an impressive creation that one has to wonder about the name Jeanne might have made for herself in the Parisian fashion industry if she had never met James, moved to Messina, and embraced a life of science.

SEWING A PLACE IN THE WORLD

Jeanne was extremely good at her new job. Stitching hats soon became stitching dresses, although we don't know whether it was Jeanne's idea or her mistress's to expand the shop's offerings. She still might have floundered—many seamstresses at the time had to take additional jobs to make ends meet—but Jeanne's diligence and artistic flair set her up for success. She rose to become the shop's director of dressmaking. While she worked, Europe continued changing around her. Napoleon met defeat at Waterloo and abdicated as emperor, and France restored its monarchy.

Luckily, everyone kept needing clothes.

In fact, in 1816 the activities of the new royal family brought Jeanne an incredible opportunity. King Louis XVIII, brother of the decapitated Louis XVI, had no sons of his own, but he wanted to make sure the crown passed to an eligible heir. He began to strengthen the monarchy by arranging marriages for all his younger relatives, including a match between his nephew, the Duke of Berry, and Maria Carolina di Borbone, a Sicilian princess. The princess needed a wedding dress, and Jeanne had made such a name for herself that she was asked to sew it.

Wearing a dress designed by Jeanne, Maria Carolina di Borbone married Charles Ferdinand. The princess lost her royal husband after just four years, when he was assassinated by a supporter of Napoleon.

The gown that Jeanne created was put on display, perhaps in the shop window. Like celebrities wearing a designer dress for one big event and then returning it to the warehouse—or, indeed, like many noncelebrity brides who have a dress custom-made for their weddings—the princess had no further use for it. But Jeanne did. She stayed nearby, no doubt taking in new business. What wealthy Parisian wouldn't want to order clothes from the seamstress who outfitted royalty?

Passersby marveled over the gorgeous dress. Many came specifically to gawk at it. A princess's wedding gown! One of the admirers was a young Irish merchant named James Power. Eager to meet the dressmaker and fluent in French, he and Jeanne impressed each other at once.

James had been living and working in Sicily, a base of operations that had been protected from Napoleon's conquest by the might of the British navy. James may have helped to provision the British ships, which relied on Sicilian ports, especially the port of Messina, to sustain them between battles. When Napoleon's empire crumbled, the Sicilian monarchy was just as eager as the French to reestablish international ties, so the marriage of Maria Carolina and the Duke of Berry served both houses well. The princess had traveled to Paris with an entourage of wealthy and high-ranking Sicilians—including James Power.

James spoke French because he'd been born in the French colony of Dominica in the Caribbean. His parents had probably moved there from Ireland in the mid-eighteenth century, when Dominica was conquered by the British (who nevertheless kept French as the colony's official language). The occupations of the Powers weren't recorded, but since the economy of Dominica revolved around coffee plantations and the import of enslaved Africans, it's a good guess that they owned a plantation.

When James was young, his father died, and his mother's remarriage eventually gave James three half siblings. So he shared with Jeanne the experience of being an older child who lost a parent and watched a new family form in the wake of tragedy.

Meanwhile, Dominica went on trading hands from English to French and back again, with varying amounts of violence. James may have disliked all the fighting, he may have disliked his new stepfamily, and he may have disliked plantation life (although he cannot possibly have disliked it as much as the enslaved people did), but for whatever reason, he left Dominica for Europe, and he eventually set up shop in Sicily.

When he traveled with the princess to Paris, did he hope that he might be lucky enough to find a bride of his own, or was his meeting with Jeanne the purest chance? Neither James nor Jeanne left a record of their first encounter, but it marked the beginning of a two-year courtship.

During this time, Jeanne concluded her work at the shop, perhaps after training a replacement. Meanwhile, James's business might have called him back to Messina, or he might have stayed in Paris until Jeanne was free to travel. One early biographer suggests that they went to England first, but all we know for certain is that on March 4, 1818, Jeanne and James were married in Messina, at the Church of Saint Luke, which still stands today.

And so Jeanne began her new life as the wife of a wealthy merchant. Here on the Sicilian coast she lived side by side with the sea in all its glory, the crashing waves and the crying gulls, the scent of salt water and the fish-filled docks. Beneath the surface, the water teemed with wondrous life-forms, from carnivorous starfish to regenerating snails to tool-using octopuses.

Gazing at the sea, Jeanne fell in love for the second time.

CHAPTER TWO

THE
EXPLORER

I have found it preferable to assure myself of facts,
because I have studied . . . not with my imagination,
but with experimental observations.
—JEANNE VILLEPREUX-POWER, 1856

Jeanne was twenty-three when she arrived in Sicily. Her mother at that age had been managing all the family's household chores, parenting a two-year-old Jeanne, and pregnant with Jeanne's first sister. It's hard to imagine that she had a moment to spare for any other interests. Jeanne, by contrast, faced a life of leisure. She had no children, and her husband's wealth turned "managing the household chores" into "supervising the servants who did the chores." In Messina, Jeanne had the chance to discover her own passion for natural history.

She pursued it with all the time and money at her disposal, and with her gifts of creativity, curiosity, and determination. While educating herself about the natural world and its methods of study, she simultaneously collected detailed data about the rocks, plants, and animals that surrounded her, cultivating a deep affection for her adopted home.

A LADY OF LEISURE

If the country of Italy, as it is often said, is a boot, then Sicily is the soccer ball the boot is poised to kick. Messina faces the toe of Italy across a narrow stretch of sea 5 kilometers (3 miles) wide. Many years after she moved to Sicily, Jeanne described the view of the island from a boat: "scenes of open hills and gently sloping beaches, covered with pasture, vineyards, gardens and olive trees, until finally its bosom welcomes the magnificent port of Messina . . . one of the most beautiful in the world."

When Jeanne arrived in 1818, did she imagine that this would be her home for the next twenty years? Or was she simply caught up in the wonder of the city? After six years in Paris, she was already accustomed to a metropolitan existence, but each city had distinct splendors. Messina's position on the sea was stunning. "A sumptuous maritime theater, or a series of buildings of uniform architecture, unfolds before the eye," wrote Jeanne. "This construction is marvelous for its vastness, spanning more than a mile [1.6 km]: it was once counted

The country of Italy as we know it today wasn't unified until 1871, the year of Jeanne's death. When she lived in Messina, it was part of the Kingdom of the Two Sicilies, so named because the island of Sicily and the southern Italian Peninsula had both previously been referred to as the Kingdom of Sicily.

This 1821 print shows the scenery around Messina that Jeanne would have encountered as she explored her new home—ancient ruins juxtaposed with daily life, an environment full of caterpillars and fossils awaiting discovery.

among the wonders of the world before being destroyed by the earthquakes of 1783. Afterwards it was rebuilt, but remains partly unfinished."

Like Paris, Messina was a city in recovery. But instead of a revolution, Messina had been wracked by natural disaster. A sequence of five earthquakes had devastated Sicily and Calabria (the region of Italy's toe) with seismic tremors and resulting tsunamis. Tens of thousands were killed—a death toll comparable to that of the French Revolution.

Although Messina's destruction had not been political, the city was no stranger to civil unrest. After the Napoleonic Wars, during which Sicily had been isolated from the rest of Italy and protected by the British navy, the Kingdom of Sicily had been reunited with the Kingdom of Naples, which covered southern Italy. (Italy would not be unified into a single country until 1871.) King Ferdinand I now ruled this joint kingdom, but he wasn't very popular among Sicilians. Maria Carolina, the princess whose wedding dress Jeanne had created, was his granddaughter. The king had hoped that her marriage would strengthen his position, but revolts sparked across the island in 1820, just two years after Jeanne moved to Sicily. The monarchy eventually stamped them out, with forceful help from the Austrian army.

Jeanne hadn't escaped the violence of revolution by moving away from Paris, but her marriage to a rich Irish merchant offered substantial protection. Although all the biographies of Jeanne emphasize the romance between her and James, the

Two years after Jeanne arrived in Sicily, revolutionaries sought to regain the island's independence. The fighting occurred primarily in the city of Palermo, some 200 kilometers (125 miles) from Messina.

fact of the matter is that we don't know how much Jeanne was motivated to marry him by affection and how much by practicality. In any case, James's support for his wife is clear. Once Jeanne had the resources and leisure to do what she liked, she threw herself into learning, and to all appearances James was equally enthusiastic about her education.

The first published biography of Jeanne, written in 1899, states that James "took [Jeanne] to his country where he gave her a careful education, to marry her later." Although this smacks of paternalism, a type of sexism that treats women as children, that perspective may betray only the bias of the biographer and not James himself. If Jeanne did indeed visit Britain before Sicily, she would have begun to learn English, and when she arrived in Messina, she picked up Italian. Latin was also added to her repertoire, perhaps as a result of her interest in the history that surrounded her. The Roman and Greek ruins of Sicily attracted tourists in Jeanne's day as much as they do today, and it would have been a thrill for her to read the ancient inscriptions on the stones. Thus armed linguistically, Jeanne set out to teach herself natural history—the careful observation and description of the world around her. She was entranced by her new island home and determined to explore and describe it in detail, from weather and rocks to plants and animals.

MARRIED
WITHOUT CHILDREN

Jeanne never had children, which was unusual for a married woman during her time. There's no writing from Jeanne on this potentially sensitive subject and no speculation, informed or otherwise, from other sources. The closest mention occurs in an article written by a professor, Alessio Scigliani, in 1837 in the magazine *Passatempo per le Dame* (the Hobby Journal for Ladies). He described Jeanne's work as an inspiration for other women: "Mrs. Power, despite so much scientific activity, does not forget about the affairs of her household, and gets along so well that she could serve as a role model for many mothers." He criticized "the pretexts that most women put forward to hide their natural indolence and the flaws in the education they have received or have not been able to acquire." To his mind, Jeanne's success showed that "you have to empower yourself to be a genius."

There's hardly a word in there that isn't appallingly sexist, not to mention classist. "The affairs of household" for the Powers would have been largely taken care of by servants. The suggestion that Jeanne could be a "role model for many mothers" suggests that Scigliani either didn't know or didn't care that Jeanne had no children. Of course, she had her pets and specimens, which perhaps required a comparable amount of attention and caretaking!

Jeanne may have been unable to have children, or she may not have wanted them. It's possible that either Jeanne or James was infertile. Infertility can be a difficult challenge to overcome even with help from twenty-first-century medicine.

Many couples today choose not to become parents, for myriad reasons, and this choice is made easier by a wide range of contraception (birth control) options. When Jeanne lived in Italy, contraception was technically illegal, but people could buy condoms to prevent sexually transmitted infections—with contraception as a side effect. Various other mechanical and chemical supplies could be sold for one purpose and used for another, and Jeanne, using her scientific knowledge and creative thinking, would likely have been able to prevent pregnancy if she wanted to. For all we know, she and James may even have had a platonic partnership, with little or no sexual activity.

For whatever reason, they were bucking the trend. They lived in a time when marriage was expected to produce babies. A lack of children was considered valid grounds for men to divorce; Napoleon Bonaparte divorced his first wife for this reason. But as far as history records, there was no such issue between Jeanne and James, who remained companionably married to the end of their lives.

A NATURALIST'S METAMORPHOSIS

Before Jeanne even set foot in Sicily, the sea crossing from the mainland may have introduced her to an almost mystical phenomenon: mirages of whole cities that appear to hover over the water. This type of mirage is called a Fata Morgana, the Italian name for the legendary enchantress Morgan le Fay, who is often associated with Sicily. As Jeanne described it,

> **Rarely, we can observe the *Fata Morgana*, which corresponds to what naturalists call *lands of fog*, or *lands of mist*: it is seen on the high seas, and often deceives the most famous navigators. . . . It consists in presenting in a pleasant and surprising way to those who are in the sea, looking at the shores of Calabria and Sicily, not just the shores, but a scene in the middle of the sea of buildings, mountains, plains, villages. It usually takes place in the summer in times of calm sea and winds, and sometimes the display is such that the sea entirely disappears, and the whole channel is occupied by an optical illusion of cities, towns, fields, and men who work there.**

These mirages are caused by warm and cold layers of air lying close together above the water and bending the light that passes through them. The illusions

This engraving published in London in 1849 illustrates the optical illusion of an apparent second city in the middle of the Strait of Messina. A Fata Morgana like this is not merely a reflection on the water surface but a distortion of light that makes us see extra copies of buildings and ships stacked on top of the real ones.

tend to move and change quickly, like the heat shimmer you see over asphalt on a summer day. As Jeanne implied, Fata Morgana mirages can be seen around the world, from California to Australia. The Sicilian name is used for them all.

In addition to such intangible marvels, Sicily hosts atmospheric phenomena that are at times all too tangible. Tornadoes spin up frequently, over land and over sea, and sometimes they cross between the two. Over the sea, spiraling between the water surface and the clouds above, they are called waterspouts. Despite the name, the funnel is mostly air filled with condensation, like a cloud. Still, it can draw up sea spray or seawater or even, in rare cases, fish. (When fish are pulled up by a waterspout, they may fall down some distance away, resulting in the extremely rare but memorable experience of "raining fish.")

Waterspouts can appear in clusters; one remarkable drawing from 1827 records nine waterspouts viewed simultaneously from a boat. When waterspouts form in fair weather, they tend to be stationary and pose little danger. When they form during storms, it's another matter. In 1851, a few years after Jeanne had left Sicily, two storm waterspouts moved onto land, destroying buildings and farmland and killing more than five hundred people.

Jeanne was fortunate to avoid such disasters as she trekked all over Sicily, cataloging what she saw. She had the advantage of being a country child, accustomed to walking. A lady born and bred in the upper class might have balked at exploring the island in this way, but to Jeanne, it was second nature. "I have traveled on foot and in all directions," she wrote, "province by province, several times all over Sicily, to gather natural history and antiquity collections." Her interests were broad, and she

As suggested by this 1827 illustration, waterspouts are fairly common off the coast of Sicily. These whirlwinds are mostly air, partly water, and typically innocuous, unless they move over land.

noticed everything. When she published a guidebook to Sicily many years later, she described a classical church in the village of Castanea with a panel of the *Virgin and Child* by the famous Renaissance painter Mariano Riccio, and a nearby church that housed a fresco by Baroque artist Litterio Paladino. Then she gushed that just around these churches, "there is no lesser quantity of insects, including beautiful butterflies, than of reptiles and rare plants." Describing statues "worthy of the gaze of the artists," she also noted that they stood on a mountain "composed of a limestone terrain with a mass of fossil shells" which she identified by name: *cardium, trochus, remus, dentalium, madrepore,* and *millepore.*

Although she cherished the whole island, Jeanne's home city of Messina held more than enough to occupy her attention. She wrote of "minerals, fossils, agates, diaspores [a type of gemstone], rare plants, migratory and sedentary birds, reptiles; in the woods near the city there are many insects, a circumstance which facilitated, during the space of 15 years, my studies on butterflies from the birth of the caterpillars to the exit of the butterfly from its chrysalis." Jeanne's particular interest in butterflies may have been spurred by the work, 150 years earlier, of the groundbreaking female scientist Maria Sibylla Merian. In the 1600s, caterpillars and butterflies were seen as unrelated animals. Merian proved that one transforms into the other, and her magnum opus, *Metamorphosis Insectorum Surinamensium,* was circulated widely and to tremendous influence throughout Europe's scientific community. Jeanne might have owned a copy herself or come across it in the home of a fellow nature enthusiast. One can imagine Jeanne poring over Merian's detailed illustration of the Sphinx moth life cycle, with egg, caterpillar, pupa, and adult all artfully arranged on the specific plant, *Annona,* which the caterpillar requires for food. How curious Jeanne would have felt about the butterflies she saw in her own travels, and how ambitious to see what she could prove!

Maria Merian presented the life cycles of insects, such as this Cluentius sphinx moth, with a combination of artistic and scientific rigor.

Jeanne went on to examine and illustrate two hundred different species of Sicilian butterflies. We can guess that the talent for artistic detail that had set her dressmaking apart now flowered in her drawings, although, sadly, none were preserved. She also documented in writing how her persistent observational approach revealed the creatures' secret habits.

She wrote,

> **For several years a species among my caterpillars never formed pupae and died. When I noticed that several of these caterpillars were no longer eating and were prowling around their compartment, I took them and left them in the countryside near a wall at the base of which there were grass; they searched among these herbs until they found what they needed. I did not lose sight of them; a few moments later, they had cut the stems of a plant which bears ears; they fixed all the small leaves of the ear on their body and united the end of the stem to the end of their body; one could not distinguish the ear which contained the caterpillar from the other ears, so well was it imitated. The caterpillars spent less than an hour in this operation; an hour later I took one of the ears by the stem; it seems that this annoyed the caterpillar because it shook itself violently; I picked up the other three and put them in their compartment which was, like all the others, numbered; I added the date. Thirty-five days later, a pretty butterfly came out of an ear, the next day two more, the fourth had died in the ear.**

With her care for precision, Jeanne wanted to identify this critical grass by name. She could not, so she described it in exhaustive detail. In reading the following, you can keep in mind that a centimeter is about the width of your fingernail, and ten millimeters make one centimeter. "Its stem is about 16 centimeters in length and 5 millimeters in circumference; the ear measures 3 centimeters in length; the heart of the ear 11 millimeters in circumference, it is covered with small somewhat concave and pointed leaves, the length of which is 7 millimeters and 2 in width, vegetates on the dry and calcareous grounds of Sicily; it was impossible for me to find it either in the Jardin des Plantes, or around Paris." (Did you figure out that this plant is about as tall as the length of your hand, with leaves a bit smaller than your fingernails?)

From the beginning of her career as a scientist, Jeanne's research was marked by a focus on living animals in their natural environment. As obvious as that approach may seem today, in the 1800s, it was almost radical.

OLD BONES AND NEW DISCOVERIES

Natural history in Europe had long been hampered by a focus on dead specimens. Naturalists, usually wealthy white men, sat indoors looking at animals that had been collected in distant lands and shipped back to Europe, dried, pinned, and stuffed. For many years, in fact, collecting unusual and attractive specimens had been a fad among the European upper class, and wealthy homes often included a "cabinet of curiosities." (In her guide, Jeanne listed for each Sicilian city collections and cabinets worth visiting, like small private museums.)

To be fair, many naturalists *had* managed to make great discoveries through their study of dead animals. Georges Cuvier, one of the most prominent paleontologists in Europe, was famous for his ability to identify nearly any bone placed before him, and he used his deep understanding of anatomy to drive a fundamental shift in the European perspective on our planet's past.

This engraving of the famous French scientist Georges Cuvier with a fish fossil emphasizes his reputation as the founding father of paleontology. His checkered legacy ranges from establishing the truth of extinction to supporting scientific racism.

Throughout Europe, there weren't any textbooks or charts marking off millions of years of history. No one had grown up playing with toy dinosaurs. The primary "textbook" was the Bible, and most people believed it was literally true, which led them to the conclusion that Earth was only a few thousand years old. They thought that every living thing had been created just as they saw it—so fossils were quite a puzzle.

We know now that bodies buried in mud or sand can be preserved, over thousands and millions of years, as dissolved minerals filter into hard parts like bone or wood and turn them to stone. Much more rarely, soft body parts like skin or feathers can be fossilized in special conditions such as a volcanic eruption. But in the 1700s, the century that ended with the French Revolution and the birth of Jeanne, most people knew fossils only as strange-shaped rocks that turned up in eroding cliffs and coal mines. Some of them looked like bones of familiar animals, such as sharks or elephants. The more mysterious ones were inexplicable.

In 1796, when Jeanne was two years old and Napoleon was still just a general in the army, Cuvier made the case for extinction: the idea that entire animal species have existed and then died out. His evidence was the differences he had found between the bones of elephants and the fossils of mammoths, proving that the latter animals were their own distinct, and *extinct*, species. A few years later, after more fossils had come to light, he proposed that Earth had once seen an Age of Reptiles, populated with dinosaurs, ichthyosaurs, and pterosaurs. He planted the first seeds of dinosaur mania, a growing interest in prehistoric beasts that would eventually lead to movies such as *Jurassic Park*, *Ice Age*, and *The Good Dinosaur.*

The logic of Cuvier's ideas, and the force with which he argued for them, won him substantial support. In 1819, as Jeanne was beginning her scientific career, Cuvier received the title baron in honor of his accomplishments. (Incidentally, Cuvier also named the group of animals, Mollusca, that Jeanne would come to know so well—the snails, clams, and octopuses.)

Cuvier lived and worked in Paris—though Jeanne probably never saw him there during her years as a seamstress—at the French Academy of Sciences, studying museum specimens. As a young man he had eagerly examined rocks and fossils in the field, but he rose to fame after he began working indoors. He developed his great theories by analyzing bones whose painstaking discovery and preparation had been completed by others, including a remarkable field scientist in England named Mary Anning.

Unlike Cuvier, whose family was financially stable enough to send him to a university, Anning had to work to support her family from a young age. Living by the sea near constantly eroding cliffs, she collected fossils to sell to tourists. She became so skillful at finding and identifying them that she gained scientific admirers throughout Europe. Although she sold fossils for the money she needed to live, she was also fascinated by the work itself. She never considered an easier or safer job, even after her beloved dog was killed by a landslide during a fossil expedition.

Perhaps the most commonly purchased of Mary's souvenirs were the ammonites, or shells built by ancient relatives of the octopus. Although these prehistoric creatures left no trace of their soft tentacles, they bequeathed us an enormous diversity of coiled shells. Some are as tiny as fingernails, and some are large enough to climb inside. Some are pearly smooth, and some are decorated with chunky bumps and needle-thin spines. Some even closely resembled the shapes of modern argonaut shells! Ammonites still abound in England's sea cliffs today. But Anning's most famous finds were the ichthyosaurs, giant marine reptiles that lived at the same time as both ammonites and dinosaurs, and contributed significantly to Cuvier's concept of the Age of Reptiles. She dug up her first complete ichthyosaur skeleton when she was only twelve years old!

Many prominent scientists relied on Anning's fossils, but because of her gender and class, they rarely credited her in their scientific publications and never admitted her to a scientific society. Posterity has begun to treat her better, as her life story inspires numerous written biographies and even a historical drama, the 2020 movie *Ammonite*.

Jeanne's scientific trajectory fell somewhere between those of Anning and Cuvier. She faced sexism, but she was rich. She could have stayed indoors as Cuvier eventually did, but she didn't want to. She was as motivated as Anning to go outside and get her hands dirty. Her privileged position due to wealth and class made it easier for her to

Fossil hunter and paleontologist Mary Anning made numerous discoveries: marine reptiles, flying reptiles, fossilized feces, and ink sacs. This painting of Anning at work also memorializes her beloved canine companion, Tray.

While dinosaurs walked on land, huge marine reptiles called ichthyosaurs swam in the seas. With her brother Joseph, Mary Anning excavated the first complete ichthyosaur fossil in 1811, and in 2015 a new species was named in her honor *Ichthyosaurus anningae*.

correspond with other scientists and demand their respect, and she was eventually able to join more than a dozen learned societies.

Jeanne became part of a new movement toward biological experimentation—observing live animals, then making and testing theories about how they lived. In addition to spending countless hours outside, Jeanne had the luxury of turning her own house into an ecosystem. She adopted several wild animals, enjoying their company as much as any devoted pet owner while recording their behavior with the keen eye of a scientist.

AN ACCIDENTAL PET

Ironically, Jeanne acquired her first unusual animal companion as a result of her intention to kill it. Although she loved to observe living animals, she also followed the standard biological practice of keeping dead animals for careful study. To preserve every detail of an organism, beyond what can be captured with drawings or descriptions, it is necessary to "fix" the entire body in chemicals that will maintain its shape without allowing it to decay or crumble. Modern scientists use formalin as a fixative, and they can order standard percentages in bulk from scientific supply companies. In Jeanne's day, there was no universal fixative and certainly no catalog with bulk pricing.

If naturalists wanted to preserve the objects of their study, they had to be chemists too. They had to obtain the ingredients and invent the recipes. They arrived at their formulations through trial and error, and the final recipe was often a closely guarded secret. We don't know how Jeanne began, whether she started from scratch or found some guidance, but we know how she ended—with a unique formulation that impressed scientists across Europe.

As Jeanne wrote, "I had composed a liqueur in which I immersed reptiles, fish, crustaceans, birds, insects, small quadrupeds and other animals, without stripping them, this liquor penetrated through their skin into their flesh, without altering the colors of scales, feathers or hair. Not only did the crustaceans retain their natural colors, but they also retained the elasticity of their limbs. Naturalists have seen large and small crustaceans in my cabinet, as well as fish, etc., etc., who looked alive, even though they had been embalmed for more than ten years. Insects never attacked any of the animals embalmed with this liquor."

Strangely enough, it was the need to mix her own formula that led Jeanne to acquire a new animal companion. "I had a tortoise which I intended to embalm, but having no liquor prepared for this purpose, I immersed it alive in a large jar of alcohol. It stayed there three days; I took it out and placed it on the floor to dry it, being careful to put a towel underneath." Jeanne assumed the three-day alcohol bath had killed the tortoise, and left its body to dry, planning to fix it later in liquor. Perhaps she got distracted with another project, or perhaps it took her longer to prepare the liquor than she'd expected. In any case, she had quite a surprise: "The next day I saw my tortoise walking quietly through my laboratory; I took her, and gave her an apple, which she ate, and some lettuce; I stroked her, scratching her neck, which tortoises like a lot."

That the animal lived may seem impossible. But tortoises are hardy. They routinely undergo estivation, a drastic reduction in metabolism that's tantamount to suspended animation. Did Jeanne know this? She wrote nothing of her astonishment and made no comment on her sudden pivot from dispassionate scientist to affectionate pet owner. Her next words about the tortoise were, "After a few days, she fell in love with me: if I went to another room, she would come there and stop by me, stretching out her head, beckoning me to scratch her neck; every day she came exactly at dessert time in the dining room, and to show that she was there, she pulled my dress until I picked up some food; I put it on a plate and gave her dessert."

Jeanne named the tortoise Mignonne (French for "cute") and found that it would come when called. To determine whether it actually recognized its name or merely Jeanne's voice, she performed a simple experiment. We can imagine her sitting in the living room with friends some evening after dinner. Mignonne has

Jeanne's tortoise was a Hermann's tortoise, which is often referred to as a land turtle. And that's not wrong—tortoises are in fact a kind of turtle, specially adapted for life on land.

stayed in the dining room, savoring the last of her dessert. Jeanne first calls to her cat, who slinks in to be pet. Still no sign of the tortoise.

"Mignonne!" Jeanne calls then. "Viens, Mignonne."

And the small brown head peeks into the room, followed by a variegated brown-and-green shell as Mignonne trundles toward her mistress. Jeanne's friends, witnessing the tortoise's recognition of her name, marvel at the sight of that hard, smooth head rubbing against Jeanne's hand, asking as clearly as the cat to be pet.

PREDATORS IN THE PARLOR

Both Mignonne and the cat (whom Jeanne never names in her writing) had departed from the household by the time Jeanne adopted a couple of pine martens. Cousins of weasels and badgers, pine martens are generalist hunters who will eat anything they can catch. In Jeanne's time, they tormented farmers, as they shared with foxes a propensity for sneaking into barns and stealing chickens.

Jeanne was intrigued by these small, furry ferocities. She acquired a couple of young martens from the forests on Mount Etna, an active volcano southwest of Messina. She kept them in her house and tamed them as humans have tamed wild animals since the Stone Age: with food. In a compendium of observations on various animals that she published in 1860, she wrote of the martens, "They took me in great friendship, began to climb on my knees, licked my hands; they followed me around the house; well, they were almost always near me."

Martens are a kind of mustelid, the largest family of mammalian carnivores. Many mustelids burrow, and some, like otters, are aquatic. Martens are unusual among mustelids in their ability to climb trees. Jeanne wanted to study this unique aspect of their behavior, so obviously, she needed a tree in her house.

James apparently had no objection—Jeanne does not even mention his thoughts on the subject—and a tree was duly installed in the anteroom. The martens climbed it at once, although they came back down to follow Jeanne when she left the room, having grown attached to the source of their food.

She gave them primarily beef but also attempted numerous other feeding experiments, which are best told in her own words.

"Shortly after the arrival of my martens, the mice we had in the house disappeared," she wrote. "However, I never observed that they caught any. I even tried to give them, at one of their meals, the flesh of a large rat; but they smelled it with a grimace, did not touch it, and walked away with an air of disgust and repugnance." No rats. But rats and mice do not inhabit trees. What about squirrels? "I got myself a live squirrel, put it on the tree. As soon as the martens saw it, they rushed on the squirrel, which, despite its agility, could not long escape the cruelty of its two enemies. The battle was short, it was caught, killed, soon torn to pieces and devoured." Could a tree also be a good place to hunt birds? Jeanne called on the children of Messina for help. "I promised them a reward if they had the skill to catch me live birds. I gave them my nets, a cage and some wheat. At the end of eight hours they brought me eleven."

What did these Sicilian youngsters think of the Frenchwoman who paid them to catch birds and kept martens on a tree in her house? They probably found her delightful. They may have wished that she would invite them in to watch the hunt, but perhaps with some expectation of how gory it would be, Jeanne did not do so. She did share the experience with two adult friends and reported that the martens, "on seeing the birds, began to climb on the tree, on the windows, on the doors, killing any that they could catch." An impressive feat for predators without wings!

Jeanne's spirit of inquiry was shared by at least one of her servants, who conducted an experiment of his own one day by showing up deliberately empty-handed when the martens expected food. He wanted to see what they would do. Jeanne reported, "At first they got angry with the servant, they made faces at him, showing him their teeth; then they came to me opening their mouths and tried to make me understand that they had not yet been given their meal. They climbed on my knees, gave me a thousand caresses, a thousand antics . . ."

The martens did not get along with more traditional pets. "If a dog were to pass, they would then take a threatening pose, their hair stood on end, they bared their teeth with grimaces and gave little grunts," wrote Jeanne. "From time to time, they also hunted cats; there was not one who dared to approach my house." They would sometimes threaten to bite humans, and Jeanne trained them out of this with a technique as old as offering food but less friendly: hitting them with a stick. Jeanne lived in a time when this was a common corrective approach not just for pets but for children, and she thought nothing of applying it to the martens. Curiously, she observed, "they never tried to bite me when I gave them a beating."

WILD ANIMALS AS PETS

Jeanne was far from the first or the last person to make pets out of wild animals. The Roman emperor Nero kept a tiger in the first century CE, and Pope Leo X acquired an elephant in 1514. During Jeanne's lifetime, the French aristocracy was fond of exotic animals, and Joséphine Bonaparte, Napoleon's first wife, kept a well-regarded pet orangutan. The habit has continued into modern times, with the Kardashians' brief adoption of a chimpanzee and Paris Hilton's more long-term commitment to her pet kinkajou (a raccoon relative).

However, in many places it is now illegal to keep exotic animals. It's dangerous for both pets and owners, and potentially for uninvolved bystanders as well. A kinkajou bite once sent Hilton to the hospital, and in the same week that Kim Kardashian shared photos of Suzy the chimpanzee, a different pet chimp was shot dead by police after mauling a friend of its owner. Wild animals can be tamed, but not domesticated.

Jeanne tamed her martens to be comfortable around humans with reward and punishment. Domestication, by contrast, takes many generations, and produces animals that are *genetically predisposed* to be comfortable around humans. It took thousands of years of selective breeding to domesticate dogs from wolves.

No matter how it is trained, a wild animal will easily revert to its wild nature. Jeanne had to constantly threaten and bribe her martens to keep her friends and neighbors safe, and it's lucky no one was ever seriously hurt. Although some places allow people to keep a pet marten even today, these mustelids still have very sharp teeth and claws that could do a lot of damage to you, your other pets, other people's pets, and backyard wildlife like songbirds and squirrels. Not to mention the furniture.

If you don't like the idea of catching a wild bird and bringing it into your house to watch it get torn apart, then a pine marten is probably not a good pet. It is also worth noting that the pine marten will not clean up after itself. Jeanne's martens would hide bird carcasses around the house to come back to later, a surprise you and your guests would probably not enjoy.

For pets, domesticated animals are the best choice. If you love wild animals, as Jeanne did, there are other ways to observe and even interact with them. Many zoos and rehabilitation centers keep them in appropriate conditions and offer work for volunteers as well as full-time employees. Meanwhile, scientists around the world study wild animal behavior, evolution, and conservation, investigating these incredible creatures in their natural habitats. This approach leads to unique observations and insights—as Jeanne would go on to demonstrate with her studies of sea life.

Many mustelids have been hunted for their fur, to the point of extinction in the case of the American sea mink and the Japanese otter. The European pine marten, pictured here, escaped such a fate and is now a protected species.

In one memorable instance, she had to use both threat and bribery to produce the desired behavior. Jeanne was busy writing that evening. Several friends came to visit, and they were turned away at the door. She described the subsequent adventure: "As they passed in the street a crazy idea came to their mind. They met one of the lantern lighters of Messina. To take his ladder, to climb on the balcony, to enter the living room, was soon done." Having guests inflicted on her by such unconventional means, Jeanne went to meet them. "As I was going to scold these gentlemen, I saw my angry martens." They usually welcomed her friends, but in this case one of the men had just returned to Messina and had never met the martens before. They were inclined to bite him, an inclination Jeanne may have sympathized with, but she wished to resolve the situation without injury. She brandished her rod to frighten the martens away, then, "I had some meat brought on a plate, I gave it to this gentleman, placing the marten on his knees, she took the meat, growling. The other marten jumped near his companion; after the meal, peace was made."

As Jeanne delighted in the wildlife of Sicily's fields and forests, the stunning beauty of the Mediterranean Sea lay always at her doorstep. She felt at least as fascinated by marine animals as by terrestrial ones, perhaps more so. But studying them was a puzzle—she couldn't go underwater, and she couldn't bring them into her house. Or could she?

CHAPTER THREE

THE
INVENTOR

*As I was the first to have the idea of studying marine animals in aquaria
or cages, I want to keep my rights as an inventor.*
—JEANNE VILLEPREUX-POWER, IN A LETTER TO RICHARD OWEN, 1857

*To Madame Jeannette Power . . . ought to be attributed, if to any one
individual, the invention and systematic application of the receptacles now
called Aquaria to the study of marine, and principally of molluscous animals.*
—RICHARD OWEN, 1858

The Strait of Messina is the narrowest passage between Sicily and the rest of Italy, a place where seawater swirls and churns in a bottleneck just a few kilometers wide. As Jeanne wrote in her guide, "Here, having crossed the Tyrrhenian waves, one arrives in Sicily, at the mouth of the strait, where the sea always makes a thunderous gurgle. The fables of Scylla and Charybdis then come to mind, and all the wonders invented by poets."

The currents here are strong and strange, bringing deep-sea creatures to the surface and nourishing underwater forests full of animals found nowhere else. As rising and falling tides force a tremendous amount of water through the narrow space, they carry nutrients from the depths into the shallow sunlit zone. This rich environment sustains an abundance of golden kelp, which in turn shelters a huge diversity of fish, crabs, corals, snails and, of course, octopuses. By the end of the nineteenth century, the strait would become the subject of intense research by zoologists from many countries. But in the 1820s, Jeanne was one of the first to study the region's marine fauna.

THE ORIGINAL HOME AQUARIUM

Even more than zoologists who study land animals, marine biologists in Jeanne's time were restricted to documenting dead specimens. It seemed obvious that there was no way for humans—who are obstinately terrestrial animals—to conduct experiments on live aquatic animals.

Pelagia noctiluca jellyfish, sometimes called mauve stingers, swarm in the Mediterranean Sea near Sicily. Jeanne may have observed them in the water or washed up on the beach. She may even have experienced their nonlethal, but painful, sting.

But Jeanne wasn't satisfied with this limitation, and she was unimpressed by the attempts of other scientists to understand dead animals. She called out one "illustrious naturalist, whom I do not wish to name out of respect," whose drawing of an argonaut "represents the octopus situated with the siphon inside the shell and the mantle towards the great opening; no doubt he had received it so. When the sailors fish argonauts, they throw

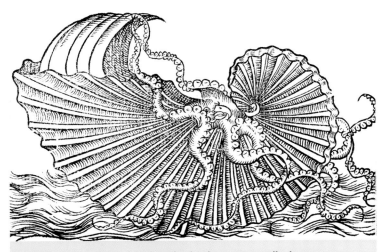

Published in 1551, Pierre Belon's book *L'histoire naturelle des estranges poissons*, which contains this unrealistic argonaut, and its sequel *De aquatilibus* were some of the first woodcuts and descriptions of aquatic life published in Europe.

them in the boat, which makes them leave the shell and die. The same people, not knowing their true position, often replace them backwards." The drawing that offended Jeanne is lost to history, but a 1551 woodcut by French naturalist Pierre Belon with its bizarre and unrealistic "toughened sail" illustrates the bewilderment of naturalists grappling with the animal's unusual anatomy.

To study marine life rather than marine death, Jeanne needed two things: a source of animals and a place to keep them alive. She got to know the fishers of Messina and would often go out on the water with them to learn their collection techniques. "This is the best conduct to be held by a naturalist," she wrote, "for obtaining fresh shells, with all the properties of their features. Those that are found on the seashore are almost never what you want, as nature makes them: the reason being that between rolling in the tides, and being exposed to rays of the sun, they are chipped by the first and discolored by the second." Marine biologists today still do some of their best work when collaborating with fishers, many of whom have lived by the water for generations and studied the sea avidly, not for abstract knowledge, but for their livelihood.

The fishers, for their part, learned of Jeanne's interest in marine life, the stranger the better, and took to saving her their rarest catches when she was not with them. "The fishermen have always been very accommodating to me," she wrote. Sometimes they invited her—through the convenient intermediary of local children—to sort through the catch herself.

The same children who caught birds for Jeanne's martens probably also liked to watch the fishing boats from the harbor, perhaps tossing their own little lines into the sea from the edge of the dock. "Bambini," a fisher might call from time to time, "Go fetch Signora Power," and a child might pass her fishing pole to a friend and race up into the city to call at the fine house of the Frenchwoman. Perhaps she hoped to catch a glimpse of the martens as she gave the message that the big nets were coming in, and would Signora Power like to see what the fishers had caught?

Jeanne might give the child a coin for her trouble, as well as compensating the fishers. After all, she had grown up working hard, first in her family's house and then as a seamstress, and would understand their position. She wrote that she paid for their catches with "a little money, or something to eat, which was more welcome to them than money."

So Jeanne had a reliable source of live animals. But if she wanted to watch them do more than suffocate and die, she'd have to provide a place for them to live—which meant she had to conceive of and create it. Her experience in the Parisian dress shop came in handy as she imagined and sketched designs. Building an aquarium would be like building a dress: cutting and assembling flat pieces into a three-dimensional shape. The material had simply changed from fabric to glass.

She was fortunate to live during the Industrial Revolution, with enough wealth to take advantage of it. Glass technology had advanced significantly around 1800, as people began using steam engines to grind and polish large plates of glass. Once Jeanne settled on a design, she most likely hired glassworkers to construct it. The result was a watertight, transparent aquarium that stood ready to receive whatever strange creatures the ocean brought to her.

Many years later, she wrote, "From 1832 to 1842 I was engaged in studying marine animals in aquaria established in my house at Messina. These aquaria were filled with sea-water, and about 1832 I gave them the name of 'cages.'" This was written in 1860, after the word *aquarium* had been coined in 1853, so that she could use it in retrospect to refer to the tools that she had called cages at the time

THE MARINE AQUARIUM, FURNISHED WITH SEA-ANEMONES, SEA-CUCUMBERS, STAR-FISH, ETC.

This engraving from the 1800s is titled "The marine aquarium, furnished with sea-anemones, sea-cucumbers, star-fish, etc." and may well have been inspired by one of Jeanne's aquariums, or a derivative of her inventions.

of their first use. Her familiarity with Latin led her to pluralize the new word after the fashion of that ancient language: one aquarium, two or more aquaria. Most of us today are less familiar with dead languages and more familiar with seeing animals in glass containers. *Aquarium* has become a comfortable English word, which we now pluralize in the English fashion: one aquarium, two or more aquariums.

Jeanne would go on to use far more than two aquariums, as she examined animals of myriad sizes, shapes, and habits—often making the first written records of their living behavior.

A WINDOW INTO A SHRIMP'S LIFE

In 1775 a Scandinavian naturalist named Peter Forsskål described a strange little "crab" from the Mediterranean Sea. He carefully counted its appendages and described each in detail, from antennae and mandibles to legs and swimmerets, and he noted the "unique architectural features" of the animal's home: "cubic, wrinkled, gelatinous, rigid, open at both ends." He recorded the animal's habit of laying eggs inside its curious home, and he named it *Cancer sedentaria*.

DEADLY DIVING DRESS

Since Jeanne had such a penchant for exploration, you may wonder why she didn't don a scuba diving suit and jump into the ocean. The problem was, diving as we know it today didn't yet exist.

That's not to say people didn't go underwater. Humans have probably been holding their breath and jumping in for as long as they've lived near the sea. Ancient people dove to collect seafood, to pry pearls from oysters, and just to pick up things that they'd dropped overboard. Salvaging shipwrecks could be particularly lucrative. However, breath-hold diving doesn't give you much time to explore, much less to conduct experiments.

To stay under longer, people needed to bring air with them. In the 1500s they began to use diving bells, simple windowless containers of wood or metal that were large enough to hold one or two people and heavy enough to sink to the seafloor. Some bells were more box-shaped than bell-shaped, but all were open at the bottom so divers could see and touch the seafloor. The air pressure inside the bell prevented water from filling it up, in the same way that you can push an upside-down cup filled with air underwater in a bathtub. The air will stay inside, as long as you don't tilt the cup. Bell divers had only a limited view of the ocean and its inhabitants, and equally limited mobility.

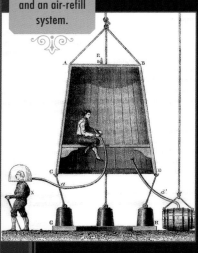

Halley's diving bell was an underwater room with a window, seats, and an air-refill system.

In 1691 Edmond Halley (of Halley's comet!) designed a bell with a window, a huge improvement. He also came up with a system of barrels to send more air down from the surface to refill the bell, as the divers consumed the oxygen in the air. Even so, diving bells weren't the safest contraptions. Another bell designer named Charles Spaulding died in 1783 when he ran out of oxygen in his own bell.

Shortly thereafter, in 1789, came the first diving suits. Divers could now wear a metal helmet fitted with small windows and riveted to a jacket. A support team on the surface pumped air from a boat down through a tube and into the helmet. By the 1820s and 1830s, divers were successfully using this system to salvage wrecks, but if anyone used the technology for science, no records exist.

This kind of diving was still dangerous. If the people at the surface forgot to pump or if anything went wrong with the pump or the hose, divers immediately ran out of air. If they couldn't get back to the surface quickly, they died.

It wasn't yet possible to compress a large amount of air into a small space, so that divers could carry all they needed with them and untether from the surface. As Jeanne was working on her aquariums, a number of other inventors were working on air compression. These experiments didn't always end well. In 1832 American engineer Charles Condert was the first successful scuba diver and the first scuba fatality. He died in New York City's East River when his breathing tube broke and his suit flooded.

It would be more than one hundred years before Jacques-Yves Cousteau and Émile Gagnan invented the Aqua-Lung, opening the way for safe scuba diving in the years to come.

In the early 1800s, other naturalists recognized the creature as a shrimp, not a crab. They identified its "home" as the body of a different animal that had been taken over by the shrimp, in some cases a jellyfish and in others a salp. (Salps are small transparent animals shaped like bulging cylinders or barrels, as gelatinous as a jellyfish but more closely related to vertebrates.) There was no uncertainty like that surrounding argonauts and their shells—this shrimp was a definite thief and in fact today it is considered a type of parasite. Naturalists in the 1800s continued to describe its anatomy in exquisite detail, an important task but not one that makes for very interesting reading, nor does it provide any information about the animal's life. Here's an example from the eminent French zoologist Pierre André Latreille: "The first two pairs of legs are attached to the two anterior segments; they are cylindrical, rather small, of five sections, the last of which almost equaling in length the three preceding ones, setaceous, small and arched. From the third segment starts a third pair of legs, a third longer than the previous ones . . ."

These studies also introduced a confusion of names. Specimens thought to belong to distinct species but later all recognized as the same were named *Phronima sedentaria*, *Phronima custos*, and *Bivonia zanzara*. That last one was described by Anastasio Cocco, a Sicilian naturalist and friend of Jeanne's. His shrimp had smaller bodies and longer antennae, features that would later be identified as marking the males of the species.

When Jeanne began to investigate the little animal that Messina fishers called *granchio con barilotto* (crab with little barrel), she would have had no reason to equate it with her friend's *Bivonia zanzara*. Neither did she recognize it as one of the *Phronima* other authors had discussed. She was less interested in its taxonomy, or naming and classification, than she was in its behavior. She placed live shrimp in their barrels into her glass aquarium, where she could watch them move. What she witnessed enthralled her.

She wrote,

> **The crustacean deposits its eggs in this barrel, which are fixed there by a gelatinous material. It enters and leaves holding its barrel with one of its arms, it hangs on it to look for its food as its young emerge from the egg. The care that this animal takes**

to prevent its young from slipping out of the barrel is incredible, it comes and goes with continual alertness, and when it searches for its food it pushes them away when they come to the edge, and catches up with them if they try to escape.

It is a constant job and requires a lot of attention from the crustacean, as the little ones are lively and often come to the edge of the barrel, which puts it in perpetual agitation. The animal does not abandon its young until they are able to obtain their food, which takes place ten to twelve days after their birth.

This text reads differently from anything written about barrel shrimp by Jeanne's contemporaries. The tale of the harried parent chasing its offspring back to safety is a drastic departure from lists of leg segments. Jeanne probably would have liked to include more anatomical detail, but she wrote, "I could not find either the drawing or the description that I had made of this little crustacean" and called her account "incomplete." Her more extensive notes may have been lost in the shipwreck, and because of this, the *granchio con barilotto* was thought to be a new species. It was named *Carcinococcus poweriae* in Jeanne's honor.

This name, like *Bivonia zanzara* and several others, is no longer used—a common fate for old scientific names, as researchers compare accounts and specimens and revise nomenclature to eliminate redundancy. But Jeanne's account remains the first, and still one of the most compelling, of its behavior. It would be over a hundred years before anyone else successfully kept these animals alive in captivity for as long as Jeanne had managed.

A female barrel shrimp (*Phronima sedentaria*) can lay hundreds of eggs. She keeps them in a pouch until they hatch and for several days after, like a mother kangaroo. Then she scoops them from her pouch into a nursery barrel.

THE EXPERIMENTAL APPROACH

Jeanne found that her indoor aquariums comfortably housed many other small animals, such as a charming sea snail called the woody canoe-bubble, whose shells grow up to 6 to 7 centimeters (2.4 to 2.8 inches) long. The snail's body is twice that long, so it can't fit inside its own shell! It's closely related to other sea snails with reduced shells and to sea slugs, which have lost their shells completely. Canoe-bubbles use their large, muscular body to dig for prey in sandy or muddy seafloors. Jeanne wanted to know what they were hunting.

Even with modern scientific tools, the quickest way to find out what an animal eats is to look in its stomach. Large animals can be induced to vomit, but small animals such as snails are typically sacrificed. Scientists can then dissect them to see what's inside. This is how Jeanne started, then, with a classical technique that did not require her clever new aquarium. She cut into the digestive tracts of the canoe-bubbles and found they were full of a mollusk called dentalia, a kind of tooth shell or tusk shell. True to their name, these animals have long, pointy shells (if it were up to me, I would have called them unicorn shells or wizard hat shells), and they pass their lives buried in mud and sand.

Now that Jeanne knew *what* canoe-bubbles ate, she wanted to know *how* they ate. She left several canoe-bubbles in her home aquarium for a day without food, to clear their stomachs of any previous meals—a technique that is now standard for experiments on feeding and predation. It ensures that all the animals are equally hungry at the beginning of a test. If you catch three snails in the sea and begin feeding them right away, and one of them eats more than the others, it could be

Because bubble snails such as *Scaphander lignarius* use their heads to burrow, they don't have the delicate tentacles typical of other snails and slugs.

because that one hasn't been able to find any food for several days, while the others gorged themselves right before you collected them. You just don't know. And if you open them up later to look at their stomachs, you don't know how much of the food was eaten during your experiment and how much was caught in the wild before you started studying them.

Once the canoe-bubbles had a chance to finish digesting whatever was in their stomachs when they were collected, and divest themselves of the undigested remains, Jeanne gave them a meal of tusk shells. But the canoe-bubbles did not slurp the animal's flesh out of its shell, as a human might eat an oyster or a snail (if your diet includes such things). They swallowed the tusk shells whole, which puzzled Jeanne. Like all snails, canoe-bubbles do not have jaws for biting and crushing, so how could they obtain any nutrition from a shell with the meaty part still tucked inside? To find out, she dissected canoe-bubbles at intervals after their feeding—one hour, three hours, five hours, seven hours.

She discovered that the canoe-bubble's esophagus contains two hard pieces that function almost like a jaw and, "facilitated by the gastric juice, reduced the *Dentalia* to a nutritive pulp." These animals can chew or grind shells *after* swallowing them!

Jeanne also performed feeding experiments on starfish, after keeping them in an aquarium without food for three days. (This starvation diet is not nearly as difficult for starfish as it would be for humans. They digest their food slowly, and may go many days in the wild without eating, only to fill up when food is available again.) At the end of the three days, Jeanne weighed and marked the starfish to keep track of each individual. Then she offered them a choice of prey items: moon snails and top snails. She was entranced by their subsequent behavior. Each starfish arranged the snails along its arms, "increasing the size of its victims to finish in the center with the biggest." After they had their meal, she weighed them again. Each starfish had consumed well over 0.2 kilograms (0.5 pounds) of snail flesh! Such a discovery would never have been possible from looking at dead starfish in a cabinet or even from observing live starfish on a walk through the tide pools.

But although starfish and snails did well in her glass aquariums, Jeanne wanted to study a greater diversity of animals. Some were too large to keep in the aquarium, and many were too particular about temperature. Jeanne was finding it difficult to maintain ideal water conditions in her home. Today, aquarium owners can use electric heaters and chillers, but nothing like that existed in Jeanne's time. Michael Faraday had only just demonstrated the first electric motor in 1821, and it wouldn't be put to practical use until the 1880s.

She had to think, quite literally, outside the box.

"GABIOLE ALLA POWER"

Although powerful currents tear through the Strait of Messina, the city is cradled in a large natural harbor, well protected from winds and waves. The water is clear and calm. It's easy to imagine Jeanne standing on the shore, gazing at the very sea her animals were fished from, and recognizing it as the perfect natural laboratory. She decided to place her new aquariums directly into the ocean, where water conditions were already ideal.

These containers could be a good deal larger than the ones she kept in her home—indeed, the bigger the better. She ended up with a design 4 meters (13 feet) long, 1.2 meters (3.9 feet) high and 1.4 meters (4.6 feet) wide, slightly smaller than a Mini Cooper car. More substantial than anything a hobbyist would keep, these were similar in size to the tanks you see at a public aquarium. She built them out of wood instead of glass and left open spaces for water to flow through. Iron held the corners together and anchored the constructions to the seafloor. She called her new aquariums *gabiole*, a derivation of the Italian word for "cage."

The water that passed between the wooden slats brought fresh oxygen and cleared out the animals' waste. And for the many organisms, such as clams and sponges, that feed by filtering tiny plankton and particles out of the water, it brought them food.

Jeanne could even combine her two styles of aquarium. To house small animals that might slip through the cracks of the large enclosure, she figured out how to suspend a glass aquarium from cords inside the large cage. The temperature of the water inside was

Of Jeanne's multiple inventions, the glass aquarium is the most recognizable and widely used today. During her lifetime, however, it was the wooden cage that was most admired by her colleagues and was named after her.

thereby maintained, and the fragile glass was both anchored and protected by the wooden cage.

How did she build these enormous structures? Jeanne had already reinvented her career several times, picking up new skills on the way, so it's plausible that she had a hand in constructing the cages herself. But she had plenty of money and her primary interest was in biology rather than engineering, so it's more likely that she paid workers to create the cages to her specifications.

Her next task was to determine a location for their installation. Jeanne summarized the process very briefly: "These I deposited (after obtaining permission from government) in a stream of sea-water which flows through the lazaretto of Messina."

The lazaretto was a marine quarantine station, named after a biblical Lazarus—not the one that Jesus brought back to life but, instead, a diseased beggar. It served a dual function, isolating ships that were considered at risk for carrying infectious disease and housing patients from Messina with plague, cholera, leprosy, or other contagious illnesses. The lazaretto's appeal for Jeanne was most likely its position on the peninsula, well outside the more active area of the port. Here she could sit in her boat over the anchored cages, relatively undisturbed by the wakes of ships coming and going.

What did the ship passengers, patients, and caretakers of the lazaretto think of Jeanne installing cages next to their hospital? It remains a historical mystery. The response of Jeanne's scientific colleagues is better documented. Her cages were considered so novel and useful that two different societies named them Power cages.

OFF WITH THEIR HEADS—AND ON AGAIN

At times Jeanne found it useful to employ both her home aquariums and her sea cages in a study, as when she began to investigate whether a sea snail can grow back a part of its body that has been cut off. This may seem like an arbitrarily cruel investigation, but the question of which animals could regenerate, and to what extent, was one of the very first shifts from observation to experiment in biology. The eminent scientist Tokindo S. Okada argued that "regeneration studies can be regarded as the origin of all experimental biology." Jeanne was familiar with the famous studies of the Italian priest and natural historian Lazzaro Spallanzani, who died just a few years after she was born. He had discovered regeneration in salamanders and showed that garden snails could grow back their head after its removal, prompting a wave of snail decapitation throughout France that preceded the later wave of human decapitation by about twenty years.

The famous French writer Voltaire was fascinated by the experiment. According to Okada, Voltaire "expressed confidence that men would one day so master the process of regeneration that they too would be able to replace their entire heads. There are many people, he implied, for whom the change could hardly be for the worse." That's still a pretty distant possibility, but the science of regeneration is providing insights that may lead to other medical applications.

Eager to find out if marine snails shared the same head-growing capacity as terrestrial ones, Jeanne brought a large snail called a triton into her home and kept it in a glass aquarium. To perform surgery on it, she hired a cutler (a person who made knives and forks before such implements could be stamped out of metal by a factory) to make her a special sharp instrument that would match the shape of the snail shell's opening. She described her procedure: "I removed the Triton from my Aquarium, I fixed it in a vise on the edge of a table, I armed myself with my instrument and waited for it to take out its head through the opening of its shell. I tried, but in vain, to remove part of its head: as the instrument approached, it withdrew so quickly that I only touched the opening of the shell; my attempts lasted four hours. Tired of the position I had to keep, I put it back in the Aquarium. The next day I started again without success; at the end, on the fifth day, I removed half of its head; it uttered a cry which gave me shivers."

The Atlantic triton snail, *Charonia variegata*, can grow over 35 centimeters (14 inches) long, making it a formidable predator of the many smaller snails, starfish, and other animals in its path.

Can a snail really cry out? Jeanne's passion for observable, repeatable facts makes it seem unlikely that she'd invent such a thing, yet the imagination can run wild, especially during a time of strong feeling—and we can imagine that Jeanne was not dispassionate about the injury she inflicted. Other scientists have never recorded sounds from marine snails, but they have documented garden snails producing a squeak of compressed air and popped mucus bubbles when withdrawing quickly into their shells. The injured triton would certainly have attempted a quick withdrawal, so perhaps Jeanne heard something similar.

She moved the snail to a cage in the sea, where it would have a suitable environment to feed and breathe as it recovered. "Eight days later, I visited my Triton," she wrote. "It showed no appearance of regeneration; I put it back in the cage and entered my home very discouraged, believing that my undertaking would not lead to any result."

But Jeanne kept the triton in its cage. Perhaps it only needed more time. She returned twelve days later, bringing her friend Anastasio Cocco, who was a doctor as well as a fellow naturalist. If the triton still had not regenerated, he could commiserate with her over the failed experiment. His human patients, after all, did not regrow lost body parts.

"Great was my joy," she wrote, "when I saw that my Triton had reproduced its cheek, its eye, its horn, and almost repaired its shell. The eye was still small and the horn was only 12 millimeters [0.5 inches] long."

To record the success, Jeanne brought the animal back to her house and drew a picture of it. Photography in the 1830s was in its earliest days, with daguerreotypes having just been invented, so illustration was the only visual documentation available to scientists. The artistic tools available for this task varied by each researcher's situation and preference. Mary Anning sketched her fossil discoveries with simple pen and ink. Maria Merian created her own paints to render butterflies in exquisite detail. Although scientists today are glad to have photography as a tool for recording data, they also continue to make regular use of illustration. Drawings can highlight important details while leaving out distractions, making them especially useful in field guides to identify species, for example.

Although Jeanne's drawing of the triton was lost, she was able to publish her detailed written results, and she went on to prove that numerous other snail species could regenerate body and shell after injury. Her interest in mollusk regeneration would become a central focus of her work with argonauts.

THE VORACITY OF THE OCTOPUS

Although they construct no wondrous shell for themselves, the common octopuses found throughout the Mediterranean intrigued Jeanne. On multiple occasions she tried to keep them in her Power cages, and found that "having devoured the Venus [clams] that I had put in for the food of my Argonauta, they went out, dragging their bodies and arms through the bars of the cage." Octopuses are known to this day as escape artists, with individuals in public aquariums crawling into neighboring tanks to snack on the inhabitants or, in the well-publicized case of Inky the Octopus, sliding right through a drain in the floor back to the open ocean. So Jeanne conducted her experiments on common octopuses in glass aquariums, either suspended from cables inside a sea cage or in her home.

To watch how these octopuses hunt, capture, and consume their prey, Jeanne offered them several kinds, including a clam called in Latin *Pinna*, in English the common pen shell. Both octopuses and pen shells are abundant throughout the Mediterranean, so it was an easy pairing to obtain. Easy to observe as well, since pen shells are commonly 30 centimeters (1 foot) or more long.

Since Cuvier named the common octopus *Octopus vulgaris* in 1797, many octopuses from all around the world have been lumped under this name. Closer inspection is revealing that the true *O. vulgaris*, pictured here, lives only in the Mediterranean and eastern Atlantic, while other so-called common octopuses are distinct enough to merit their own scientific names.

Unlike a canoe-bubble, the octopus cannot swallow its shelled prey whole—it does not have a grinding esophagus to render it into "nutritive pulp." Instead, octopuses rely on other parts of their anatomy. The powerful suction cups on an octopus's arms can pry open shells, or its rasping tongue can drill a hole in the shell, through which the octopus can spit venom that loosens the clam's muscles until the shell falls open.

TOOL USE
IN ANIMALS

Before Jane Goodall observed tool-using chimpanzees in the 1960s, most scientists were certain that only humans used tools. Since then, dozens of species, from wasps to pigs, have proved otherwise.

Dolphins protect their noses with sponges while foraging on the seafloor. Finches use cactus spines to hunt for insects. Raptors carry burning sticks to spread wildfires that flush prey out of hiding.

It's also worth remembering that people *have* observed tool use in nonhuman animals since antiquity, but these observations were frequently ignored or forgotten. Thousands of years ago, the Roman naturalist Pliny recounted a now-famous story of thirsty, tool-using crows.

As the story goes, the crows found a pot with water in it, but the water was too deep for them to reach with their beaks. Instead, they brought stones and dropped them into the pot, raising the water level high enough for them to drink.

This fable was validated in 2009, when researchers set up four rooks (cousins to crows) with containers of water. They didn't want to deprive the crows of water to make them thirsty enough to innovate, so they added the appeal of a worm floating on top of the water in the containers. The rooks, who had never been exposed to a task like this, quickly started grabbing stones and tossing them in, then grabbed the delicious worms as the water level rose.

Solving such complex problems with tools has so far only been seen in birds and primates. But is that because we haven't yet figured out how to test animals whose habits and habitats are less similar to our own? What would be the equivalent study for an octopus?

Scientists have seen octopuses using tools in the wild. Many species build dens for themselves, protecting the entrance with deliberately placed stones and shells. One species, now known as the coconut octopus in honor of its curious habit, carries empty coconut husks around as a mobile shelter. Meanwhile, in laboratory aquariums, octopuses show an astonishing capacity to manipulate objects such as jars, boxes, plugs, and rods in a quest for tasty treats. It may be the creativity of humans, rather than that of octopuses, that still limits our understanding of these animals' capabilities.

A thirsty crow who couldn't reach the water in a pot dropped in pebbles to raise the water level.

Jeanne discovered that the octopus can also use its wits. Pen shells are filter feeders, swishing seawater through their bodies to eat the plankton it carries, and the octopuses seemed to know that pen shells would have to open up to eat sooner or later. When Jeanne wrote about it, she referred to the octopus as a cephalopod, the broader term for the group of animals that also includes squids and cuttlefish. "One day when I was observing my animals, I noticed that the cephalopod was holding a piece of rock in one of its arms, and was watching for the Pinna, which opened its valves; when they were fully opened, the cephalopod, with incredible skill and promptness, threw the stone that it held between the valves of the Pinna, which prevented the latter from closing them, and the cephalopod began to devour the mollusc."

Like Jeanne, the octopus had made a task easier by developing a tool. Jeanne had invented aquariums to observe sea creatures; the octopus invented a rock wedge to procure food. At the time, most scientists didn't believe that any animals other than humans were capable of using tools like this.

The Roman naturalist and historian Pliny the Elder had recorded a similar account of an octopus wedging open a shell with a pebble. However, neither his ancient records nor Jeanne's report were scientifically rigorous. They constituted casual observations rather than precise, replicated experiments. Modern scientists studying octopus behavior have not yet found further evidence for this particular type of tool use, although it remains plausible.

"It would require whole pages to describe all the stratagems employed by the octopus for the capture of his prey," wrote Jeanne. "I should have to tell things which would appear incredible; and his voracity is such, that notwithstanding the abundance of nourishment with which I furnished him, I was compelled to remove him from the cage, or he would have devoured all my Mollusca." Probably having heard fantastical stories from sailors, Jeanne also reported, "So great is its voracity, that it even attacks man, tears away his flesh, and eats it."

She gave no specific accounts, however, and she may have been merely referring to tall tales she had heard around the port. She herself seemed undeterred from taking on these fearsome creatures as research subjects.

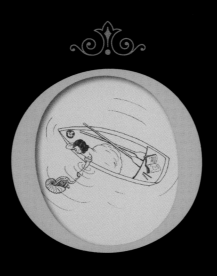

CHAPTER FOUR

THE
DETECTIVE

*I never thought of renouncing my enterprise, although I saw my
repeated attempts fail to produce any satisfactory results. I armed myself
with patience and courage, and it was only after several months that
I succeeded in clearing up my doubts, and at the same time seeing my
research crowned with happy success.*

—JEANNE VILLEPREUX-POWER, 1856

Argonauts, the octopuses, are named after Argonauts, the mythical sailors, who were named after their equally mythical ship, the *Argo*. As the ancient Greek story goes, these Argonauts followed their captain, Jason, in his quest for the Golden Fleece to secure his rightful kingship. They sailed all over the Mediterranean having exciting and horrific adventures, and there doesn't seem to be any earthly reason you'd want to name a shell-dwelling octopus after them.

But at one time people believed that argonaut octopuses were themselves little sailors. Separated from its shell, an argonaut looks much like any other octopus except for two of its eight arms, which trail enormous membranes like flags—or sails. And the shell itself does look somewhat like a boat. Taking these two facts together, classical writers imagined argonauts bobbing along the sea surface, arms in the air and shell in the water.

In 79 CE, the naturalist Pliny (the one with the stories of pebble-wielding octopuses and crows) described an argonaut like this: "Extending backwards its two front arms, it stretches out between them a membrane of marvelous thinness, which acts as a sail spread out to the wind, while with the rest of its arms it paddles along below, steering itself with its tail in the middle, which acts as a rudder."

The human protagonists of the book *Twenty Thousand Leagues under the Sea* observe a school of unrealistically "sailing" argonauts from the top of their submarine . . . which is named, humorously enough, the *Nautilus*.

This is balderdash, not least because octopuses of all species lack tails. (Possibly he was referring to the animal's mantle.) Pliny does deserve some credit for attempting to cover, in his monstrous thirty-seven-volume work *Natural History*, everything about the world from stars to stones, agriculture to medicine, elephants to bees. He recorded an abundance of both accurate facts and tall tales. While today we're interested in determining which is which, throughout medieval Europe, people were more inclined to accept and repeat the ideas of an ancient authority like Pliny than to go out and test them.

The range of argonauts themselves extends well beyond European waters. They can be found all around the globe, as long as the water is not too cold. However, they rarely venture close to shore—with the Mediterranean and Sicily, in particular, appearing to be exceptional in that regard. In most places, humans would be far more likely to encounter an empty argonaut shell washed up on the beach than a living animal. The Hawaiian language has several names for the shells: ‘au-wa‘a-lā-lua, ‘aumoana, moamoa, and moamoa wa‘a. In Japanese the shells are named aoi-gai for their resemblance to half of the leaf of an Aoi plant, while the animals themselves are kaidako, or shell octopus. Unfortunately, any ancient legends or hypotheses about argonaut biology from outside of Europe have proven intractably difficult to fish up from the depths of history.

Jeanne's observations would prove that argonauts do not use their arm membranes as sails, any more than they use their shells as floating boats. In the process of tackling the age-old question of whether argonauts make or steal their shells, Jeanne clarified many aspects of this curious animal's biology—from the development of its grape-cluster eggs to the identity of its missing males.

A SHELL LOST AND A SHELL REGAINED

If you could ask any predator in the ocean, they'd tell you that octopuses are squishy and delicious. With no bones and a body of solid muscle, they make a perfect protein-filled meal. Not surprisingly, octopuses have evolved sophisticated defenses against predators, from ink clouds to instantaneous camouflage. And they're not too proud to use one of the oldest tricks in the book: hiding in a hole. Being boneless, they're good at it.

Because octopuses can squeeze through any opening that fits their hard beak, they hide easily in rocks, in empty coconuts, in cans and bottles and other human garbage, and in every kind of shell. Clam shells, snail shells, lobster shells, you name it. If the shell isn't already empty, they're likely to eat whoever's inside and then take up residence. Octopuses have probably been hiding in other animals' shells ever since they lost their own.

Wait. Octopuses used to have their own shells? Well, yes, at least, their ancestors did.

Octopuses belong to a group called cephalopods, which are part of a larger group called mollusks (named by Cuvier, as you may recall). The word mollusk comes from the Latin word for "soft," and these animals all have a soft, squishy body called a mantle. More than five hundred million years ago, mollusks began to secrete minerals and proteins from their mantles to produce a hard shell that would protect their squishiness from predators. The strategy worked so well that it has survived to the present day. Mollusks include all the world's snails, clams, and mussels—nearly every seashell you can think of. The main building blocks of all these shells are tiny crystals of calcium carbonate, which the animal creates by drawing raw ingredients from the surrounding water. When cephalopods first evolved as a distinct group of mollusks, they grew shells with their mantles too.

A SAMPLING OF MOLLUSKS

Banana slug

Blue glaucus

Giant clam

Blue mussel

Common octopus

Veined squid

Today, only one kind of cephalopod still grows a typical molluscan shell: the chambered nautilus. Like a snail, the nautilus's mantle is fully connected to its shell. To pry either snail or nautilus from its shell is to tear its flesh and inevitably kill it. But the nautilus's cousins, octopus and squid, gradually stopped growing shells over millions of years. Similar to the way our primate ancestors lost their tails for ease of walking upright, the ancestors of octopuses and squids lost their shells for faster, more efficient swimming. The squid's shell eventually became a slender internal rod that supports a streamlined lifestyle of pure speed. The octopus's shell became nothing at all.

The argonaut is clearly an octopus. It looks like an octopus, swims like an octopus, and inks like an octopus. But while other octopuses readily hide inside empty seashells, they do not insist on carrying shells everywhere with them. An argonaut is as devoted to her shell as a two-year-old to a beloved blankie. But she is not literally attached to it the way a nautilus is. Still, over the years scientists have wondered if she could be some kind of nautilus. Argonauts are even sometimes called paper nautiluses because their shell is so thin, pale, and delicate.

In fact, to be thorough with the history of names, we must take a step back. Chambered nautiluses live in the tropical Indo-Pacific, so Europeans during the classical era had never seen them and had no name for them. The Greek name *nautilus*, which means "sailor," was actually given to the Mediterranean-dwelling

Scientists think there are about six living nautilus species, with twenty-five hundred more known from the fossil record. Awkward swimmers with poor eyesight, nautiluses are also fantastic shell-builders with an incredible sense of smell.

argonauts before they were ever called argonauts. Later, when Europeans began to see the shells of chambered nautiluses imported from the tropics, these shells reminded them of argonaut shells, and so they called them nautiluses too. The descriptors "chambered" and "paper" were used to distinguish between the two. In 1758 the father of taxonomy, Carl Linnaeus, gave the paper nautilus a Latin name, *Argonauta argo*, and scientists began to use this when referring to the animal. Over time, "paper nautilus" has fallen out of usage, so we can stick with the name argonaut from here on.

The beautiful mysteries of the argonaut captivated Jeanne, and she would spend over ten years investigating them. She knew that scientists couldn't agree on the origin of the animal's shell. One would insist that if a nautilus can build a shell, then so can an argonaut. Another would counter that an argonaut could not build its shell because it is not shaped like its shell. This insistence that an animal could only build a shell to match its own body shape, however, was a mere untested hypothesis.

"I perceived that lack of experience was the cause of these different opinions," Jeanne wrote, presumably tired of naturalists quoting Pliny without doing any original investigation. "Everything should be cleared up, if one conducted thorough research on this interesting point."

A METHODICAL APPROACH

Jeanne's determination to study living animals came with plenty of challenges. If you're studying preserved specimens, you can set them aside for a while to collect martens on Mount Etna or catch butterflies in churches, but if you're studying live animals, then you'd better stay home and keep them fed. Especially if they're octopuses, because octopuses are *hungry*.

Jeanne caught food for the argonauts herself, having learned from the sailors of Messina how to fish with an *angamo*, which she described as "a net bag . . . attached to a piece of straight iron, flattened and serrated like a rake, with a rope on each side." The *angamo* was dropped from a boat and dragged by its ropes along the seafloor, where the rake pulled plants and animals loose and the net collected them—similar in shape and function to a modern trawl net. From this haul, Jeanne prepared banquets of chopped shellfish and squid for her argonauts, and as they learned to recognize her, they would swim up and take pieces of food from her hands.

The Messina harbor, as portrayed in this 1868 painting, offered Jeanne an ideal natural laboratory—clear and shallow, somewhat sheltered from the wilder weather of the open sea, full of animal life and the boats and fishing gear needed to catch it.

Jeanne probably began by keeping argonauts in her home. However, she struggled with the animals' sensitivity to their environment and the difficulty of providing the habitat they needed indoors. Even today, with a wealth of modern aquarium technology, octopuses are still finicky pets. Jeanne was determined to do things right. "We must be careful to operate in the sea itself," she concluded, "because it is essential that the temperature of the water remain constant."

In addition to climate control, the ebb and flow of the sea provided a natural cleaning service for Jeanne's aquariums. This was necessary because octopuses tend to love privacy, and if you invade that privacy, they're liable to squirt ink. Not only do ink clouds block the view of the eager scientist, but an octopus can die if it breathes its own ink for too long. The tides and currents washing through Jeanne's in-ocean Power cages took care of that problem.

Jeanne discovered that ink wasn't the argonauts' only defense. She writes of "another ploy" these octopuses used, when she reached into the cage to catch them in her hands: "They poured violently against my face a quantity of water by means of the siphon." The siphon is a bit of anatomy universal to all cephalopods. It's how they breathe, by pulling seawater into their mantle so their gills can extract oxygen, and it's also how they produce the water jets that propel them forward when swimming. As Jeanne learned, these jets of water have additional uses—aquarium octopuses to this day are known to squirt water at things and people they don't like. (One octopus is even supposed to have extinguished a too bright ceiling light with a well-aimed squirt.)

Hour after hour, year after year, Jeanne sat in her boat, occasionally drenched with water by cranky argonauts, watching and recording her observations. At least she had a warm and beautiful place to work. "The sea is so transparent and so clear in Sicily, that it is very often easy to distinguish small objects at great depth," Jeanne wrote. "And when the water was a little agitated, I calmed it and made it become like ice in an immense circle around my boat, with wet sand well mixed with oil that I threw by handfuls to the right and left."

But there were storms too large to be calmed by oil, and on at least one occasion, bad weather broke her cages, releasing her argonauts to the four winds (or rather, the four and more ocean currents). Undeterred, Jeanne restored the cages and caught replacement argonauts. Over the years, she examined more than one thousand individuals, carefully replicating each experiment to be sure of consistent, reliable results.

GETTING TO KNOW THE ARGONAUT

One of Jeanne's earliest experiments was one of the simplest. Knowing that argonauts could climb out of their shells and back in again, Jeanne wondered if they would use this ability to escape. Power cages had openings large enough for an octopus unencumbered by a shell to slip through. But unlike common octopuses, her argonauts never took advantage of this getaway scheme. It seemed that they were more motivated to remain with their shells than to return to the wider ocean—especially, one imagines, once they became accustomed to regular meal delivery.

The patient hours that Jeanne spent in her boat above her cages, watching and waiting, were rewarded with remarkable sights. The translucent shell of an argonaut is lovely enough, lined with delicate ripples like sand under shallow water, but it becomes something else entirely when the animal inside stretches out and covers it with the membranes of her arms. Her skin spills over the shell like liquid silver, full of tiny reflecting cells as well as color-changing organs that add layers of red and pink and purple, dots of color expanding and contracting, altering her appearance moment by moment.

CALMING WAVES WITH OIL

Have you heard the expression "pouring oil on troubled waters"? It means "calming a difficult situation"—for example, making peace between quarreling friends—but it has a literal origin. Sailors have been trying to flatten waves with oil since ancient times. It might seem like a superstitious attempt to appease a mercurial sea, but you can bet that Jeanne wouldn't have kept doing it if it didn't work. She may have learned the trick from Sicilian sailors, or she may even have read Benjamin Franklin's scientific investigation of the phenomenon, published twenty years before her birth.

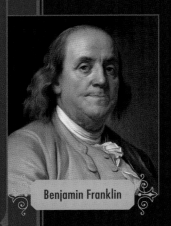

Benjamin Franklin

Oil and water are well known for repelling each other. That's why you can pour them both into a jar, shake them up, and then watch them separate into a layer of lighter oil floating on a layer of heavier water. The explanation lies in their molecules, the minuscule bits of matter that make up a substance. Oil molecules are usually described as hydrophobic, which literally means "afraid of water," or in chemical terms, unable to mix with it.

But many oils, such as the olive oil Jeanne probably used, are more complex. They contain molecules with one hydrophobic end and one hydrophilic (water-loving) end. These molecules are called amphipathic, though the terminology is less important than the fact that such molecules are both attracted and repelled by water. If you pour them onto the sea, each molecule orients itself with the water-loving side in the water and the water-fearing side out of it, spreading the oil into a blanket one single molecule thick.

Franklin wrote in 1773, "Now I imagine that the wind, blowing over water thus covered with a film of oil, cannot easily catch upon it, so as to raise the first wrinkles, but slides over it, and leaves it smooth as it finds it."

Over the years, the effect of oil on water has never ceased to fascinate scientists, and in 2007 a group published an incredibly detailed description of the mechanism behind it. When wind blows over water, it tries to push the water into waves, but these waves compress the molecules in the oil layer, which resists compression and pushes back against wave formation.

Pouring oil on a stormy sea isn't going to suddenly flatten huge whitecaps, but it does an impressive job of smoothing the ripples Jeanne had to contend with in the port of Messina. As for the sand that she mixed with the oil, it was probably a way to add weight and grip. It's easier to throw a handful of sand than a handful of oil. Once the oily sand hits the water, the components separate: the heavy sand sinks and the oil floats.

Since the days of Franklin and Jeanne, this technique has fallen out of use. We have so many other ways to see underwater now, from glass-bottom boats to scuba gear to submersibles and robots—plus, oil slicks have earned a bad rap over the ensuing century and a half. Most of us have seen pictures of the widespread destruction caused by industrial spills, and although vegetable oil isn't as toxic as petroleum, it can still harm wildlife by matting fur and feathers, coating eggs, and altering the oxygen and nutrients in the water as it biodegrades.

"When the air is calm, the sea is calm, and she thinks herself unobserved, it is then that the argonaut adorns herself with beauties," Jeanne wrote. "But I had to be prudent to enjoy her rich colors and graceful pose, for this animal is very suspicious, and as soon as she perceives that she is being observed, she hides in the twinkling of an eye."

Argonaut shells are much thinner than other seashells—so thin that Jeanne wondered if the argonauts could see through them. She noticed that they often rested and swam about with their eyes tucked inside their shells. When she moved a stick through the water toward these shell-covered eyes, the argonauts jetted away, so she concluded that the shell was more window than wall.

The delicacy of the argonaut shell has always been obvious to collectors. Anyone who finds one washed up on a beach will also find that the utmost care is required to transport it anywhere without fracturing it. How could an animal live in such a fragile shell? Wouldn't it be constantly broken by the movement of the sea? Jeanne pressed on a shell underwater and found it flexible. Curious whether the water caused the flexibility, she took a dry shell from a dead animal and soaked it. Three days' immersion rendered it "almost as flexible as the first." The shell, she showed, is delicate only when dried. In its natural environment, it's robust.

These little tests were mere warm-ups for Jeanne's overarching question: Is the argonaut a builder or a thief? She decided to approach this study from the

This dried shell of a greater argonaut, *Argonauta argo*, is fragile and white—the only way many naturalists had ever seen it. Jeanne observed that argonaut shells underwater are flexible and translucent.

beginning of the argonaut's life. The well-known Italian naturalist Giuseppe Saverio Poli claimed to have seen argonaut embryos with shells inside their eggs. If true, this observation would be solid support for the builder theory. Alas, he had died nearly a decade before Jeanne began her work, so she couldn't ask him for details. She could, however, repeat his experiments.

BABY'S FIRST SHELL

All argonauts with shells—in other words, all the argonauts that anyone in Jeanne's time had seen—are females. During breeding season, they lay eggs inside their shells and keep them safe, clean, and well oxygenated with water movement. In this regard, argonauts follow the octopus rule book, since all octopus mothers find a safe place to lay their eggs and watch over them until hatching.

However, in most species of octopus, mothers stop eating once they've laid eggs and die soon after their babies hatch. They have only one spawning season, at the end of their lives. But argonaut females reproduce multiple times throughout their lives, a rare trait among octopuses.

This repeated reproduction gave Jeanne ample opportunity to extract argonaut eggs from their mothers' shells. She cleared away the jellylike material that surrounded the eggs and studied the embryos under a microscope (already a common tool for scientists in the 1800s). "The little octopus which has just been born has no shell, and I conclude that there is none in the egg," wrote Jeanne. "Poli's observations do not correspond to mine, and if it were not a man so famous, I would dare to say that the tunic [membrane] of the egg was taken for the supposed germ of the shell."

This was a clever way to overturn the work of an eminent scientist without sounding too critical. Whatever it was that Poli had seen, he interpreted it as what he was looking for—an enduring habit of humans throughout history. (Christopher Columbus famously claimed in 1492 that the Caribbean islands he encountered were the "Indies" he sought.) However, humans have also been aware of this tendency for a very long time. Two hundred years before Jeanne, the scientist Francis Bacon wrote, "The human understanding when it has once adopted an opinion . . . draws all things else to support and agree with it." Today we call it confirmation bias, and we've designed experiments to study it and techniques to mitigate its negative effects—all with the same weird and amazing human brains

The translucence of the argonaut shell and its service as a brood chamber are both apparent in this photograph, taken during a night dive, of a female brooding small clusters of eggs.

that produced the bias to begin with.

It's only fair to report that Jeanne was no exception to such human foibles. Later on, we'll see her mistakenly identify a mouth and an intestine in the middle of a simple arm.

In any case, Jeanne had proven that argonauts hatch without a shell. What next? She continued her careful observations through the first days of their life, during which they remain with their mother. To her great delight, she noticed the earliest stages of shell growth in two-day-old argonauts. She saw a tiny octopus with its two membranous arms curled into the exact spiral shape of a shell, and "not wanting to disturb it [further]" Jeanne returned it to its mother. "Five or six hours later, I retrieved my octopus, and found that the little one had already begun its shell."

The baby argonauts were growing their shells with their *arms*. The membranes themselves were secreting the material of the shell, creating crystals of calcium carbonate. This neatly resolved the objection of some naturalists that an argonaut's body did not match its shell shape, for the main body of the animal had nothing to do with the secretion of the shell. It was a remarkable discovery, though not wholly unexpected, as those bizarre arms had to be good for something. But this was the first cephalopod and the first *mollusk* ever to be seen producing a shell without using its mantle—and it remains so to this day. The argonaut is a true octopus.

This young female argonaut, photographed in the Philippines, will need to grow her shell significantly larger before she can lay and brood eggs inside it.

Like all other octopuses, it is descended from ancestors who lost the ability to grow a shell from their mantles. Then, unlike all other octopuses, argonauts reevolved a brand-new way to make a shell. And it's a lot faster than shell making with a molluscan mantle.

"One must see the octopus working to get an idea of the speed it puts into the construction of its shell, especially at the beginning," wrote Jeanne. It took only a few hours for these babies to construct their shells, and then they left their mothers to strike out on their own.

To see if the babies could produce shells away from the protection of the mother and her shell, Jeanne devised yet another clever container, this one to keep babies in place while allowing water to flow through. Unfortunately, the tiny argonauts thus contained didn't survive. She also tried to put eggs into this container to see if they would develop and hatch without the mother and that, too, was impossible. "I have no doubt that the octopus takes care of the development and preservation of small octopuses and eggs, and that it preserves them from contact with water by covering them with a gelatinous substance," she reported. One hundred years later, scientists remain unable to rear argonaut eggs separate from their mother, although this tricky feat has been accomplished for several other species of octopuses.

Adult argonauts, as Jeanne found with a series of heartrending experiments, were also doomed by forced separation from their protective shell.

PATCHWORK MENDING

Although adult argonauts can crawl out of their shells, Jeanne had already seen that the animals would not willingly abandon their delicate coiled homes. Now she removed the shells herself to see if the argonauts could construct new ones, but these hopes were dashed. She describes the shell-less creatures sympathetically: "These poor animals were very anxious, looking in all directions in the cage for their shell. I could see they were not used to swimming without their shells." They never grew a new shell and died within days.

But Jeanne knew that adult argonauts could secrete new shell material from their arms. She had already observed, during the breeding season, that they would regularly enlarge their shells to make room for eggs and hatchlings. If they couldn't make a new shell from scratch, perhaps they could repair a broken one.

These studies were also a rather sad affair. In September 1833, of twenty-seven

Argonauts display a tendency to cling to other animals and objects they encounter. This juvenile argonaut rides a fallen leaf 21 meters (70 feet) below the ocean surface.

THE ETHICS OF ANIMAL EXPERIMENTATION

The amount of injury and death that Jeanne inflicted on her argonauts is not comfortable to read about. She doesn't shy away from it—she compares the fragility of argonauts to the sturdy nature of the common octopus by reporting, "If [the argonaut] is irritated, it becomes furious. . . . I saw it die of irritation. Common octopuses are nowhere near as sensitive; after tormenting one for three hours and cutting off two of its arms, it survived." She wrote too about feeding her pine martens with live birds and being entertained—"though not the poor birds"—by the gruesome hunting spectacle that followed.

Jeanne felt a great deal of empathy for the animals she studied on land and in the sea. At the same time, she wanted to learn how they lived and how their bodies worked, which led to predator-prey studies of pine martens and birds and experiments on argonauts with broken shells and damaged arms.

Today many people strongly oppose scientific experimentation on animals. This sentiment is fueled by a history of scientists glossing over the extent of their animal studies. Science does itself no favors by dismissing the animal pain that has been central to such experiments as Pavlov's famous study on dog drool. We often learn only that Ivan

Ivan Pavlov, recipient of the 1904 Nobel Prize for Physiology or Medicine

Pavlov taught dogs to salivate at the sound of a bell without learning that he took his measurements by cutting openings into the dog's throat and all along its digestive system. He wrote about his frustration when the animals died "as a result of extended starvation and a series of wounds." Ignoring this dark history only feeds the suspicion that something bad is still being hidden.

Yet we all benefit tangibly from lab animal sacrifices. Medical science, with its delicate surgeries and miracle drugs, exists because of foundational research on countless lab mice, rats, rabbits, and other animals. Even our best efforts toward nature conservation rely on information about how and where different species live, which requires collecting, sampling, and sometimes killing animals. In places where non-native species, such as cats or rats, put native species at risk of extinction, conservation efforts actively focus on killing off these "pests."

The ethical questions raised by these situations are complicated by our ideas about what constitutes pain and whether animals feel it. At the time of Jeanne's work, many people still argued that not all humans felt pain (this was one of the justifications for slavery in countries where it was still legal, including the United States) and there were no

Ivan Pavlov's dogs were subjected to conditions that would be considered unethical today.

animal rights activists. Modern neuroscientists have a working definition of pain: an internal state of distress that results when your senses detect damage to your body. It's difficult to study, though, because just about any animal with nerves will move away from something that causes damage. That simple response doesn't prove it's experiencing distress.

It's easy to understand how some species elicit more sympathy than others, and most people don't think insects and jellyfish need to be protected at the same level as dogs and horses. Thus, although many countries have passed laws against animal cruelty, not all animals are protected. Until 2010, legal protection covered only animals with backbones, with the notable exception of 1993 UK legislation that extended protection to octopuses. In all other nations, octopuses were on their own, along with snails, jellyfish, sponges, and the rest of Earth's glorious invertebrate life-forms.

In the last few years, movements to protect animals more broadly have emerged, and the cephalopod research community is now prioritizing humane treatment of its subjects. In 2021 a sophisticated test that had been used to demonstrate pain in mammals showed the first evidence for pain in an invertebrate: octopuses. Anesthetics, or pain-relieving medications (like Tylenol for cephalopods), are increasingly available and required for operations like Jeanne's.

Much of the latest research on octopus anesthetics comes from laboratories in Sicily, Jeanne's adopted home. If she were still working there today, she would probably be an active participant, eagerly developing new techniques for the humane study of her beloved octopuses.

argonauts whose shells Jeanne broke, only four survived. These survivors, however, along with others in later experiments, showed a wondrously clever approach to mending their shells. They would take one of the broken shell pieces Jeanne had left in the enclosure and weld it into the gap in their own shell. Examining the repair job chemically, Jeanne found that argonauts attached their patches with the same substance they used to grow their shells from scratch.

Jeanne noted how both the arm membranes of an argonaut and the membranous mantle of a cowrie often stretch around the outside of these animals' shells. Although for hundreds of years, naturalists had been repeating Pliny's claim that an argonaut uses its membranes as sails, Jeanne was certain that the main purpose of the membranes was to maintain the shell. She proved this hypothesis by cutting the membranes and observing the effect on shell growth. If the left arm membrane was cut, shell growth and repair on the left side suffered; a comparable effect could be produced on the animal's right side. The argonaut continues to work on her shell throughout her life, fixing any damage and enlarging it as needed to fit her growing body and eggs.

The argonaut's careful construction and repair work may have reminded Jeanne of her own work as a seamstress. Perhaps her admiration for the animal was influenced by her years of diligent dressmaking. Surely she saw in the argonaut's shell a wonder to rival or surpass the wedding gown of a princess. "When the rays of the sun shine on them," Jeanne wrote, "along the hull can be seen a band of shape and colors like the rainbow. That's when her pose is really beautiful."

Because cowry shells are constantly covered by extensions of the mantle, they are some of the smoothest seashells around and have been used in jewelry and as money for thousands of years.

THE MALE OF THE SPECIES

A persistent question about argonauts remained: If every argonaut is found with a shell, and if every argonaut with a shell is or will one day become a mother—where is the male of the species? Where are the fathers?

Some scientists had speculated that male argonauts, lacking shells and arm membranes, were simply indistinguishable from the common octopuses of the area, but Jeanne found this argument unconvincing. She had placed numerous common octopuses into the cages with her argonauts and saw they would have nothing to do with each other. "It was useless to make these experiments," wrote Jeanne in exasperation, already forming a different hypothesis about male argonauts. She thought they might be much, much smaller than the females—and hiding in plain sight.

Jeanne was not the first to observe the small, arm-shaped "parasites" that seemed always to be present among the eggs of a brooding female argonaut. In 1829 Cuvier had described one such parasite as a worm and gave it a new Latin name, *Hectocotylus octopodis*. Referring to the line of suckers found on the creature, the name can be translated as "hundred-cupped thing from an octopus." Not wrong but also not exactly right.

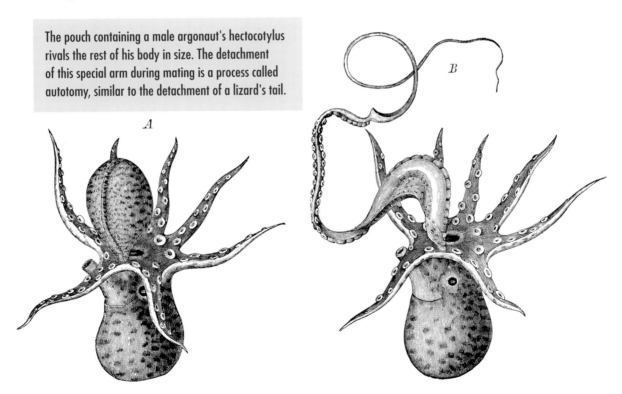

The pouch containing a male argonaut's hectocotylus rivals the rest of his body in size. The detachment of this special arm during mating is a process called autotomy, similar to the detachment of a lizard's tail.

Since scientists before her had seen the hectocotylus as an entire animal, Jeanne expected to see the same and even thought she could identify its mouth and intestine. But she was certain it must be a cephalopod rather than a worm. After thinking long and hard, she came to a conclusion that had eluded all other argonaut observers before her—this hectocotylus must be the male argonaut. After all, its appearance was so very similar to an arm of the female argonaut that it could easily belong to the same species, and when dissected, it always contained sperm.

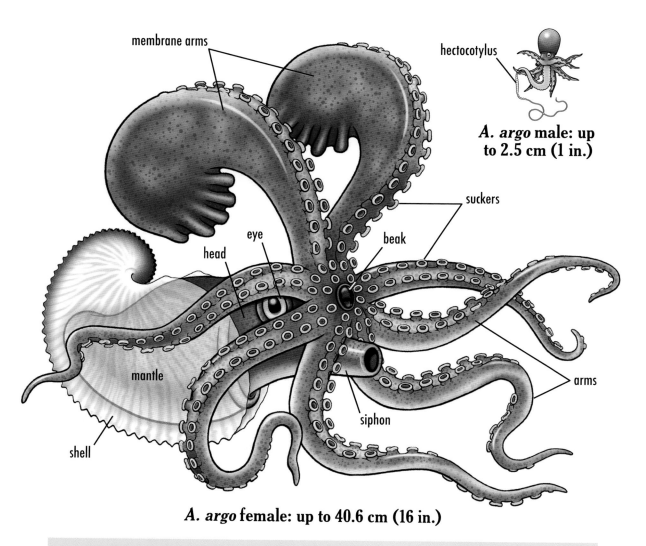

A. argo male: up to 2.5 cm (1 in.)

A. argo female: up to 40.6 cm (16 in.)

The most striking features of argonaut anatomy—the female's membranes and shell and the male's hectocotylus—are quite apparent in this anatomical diagram. It's equally interesting to note that the rest of their anatomy is standard-issue octopus.

Jeanne suggested that these males must hatch directly from the eggs. How curious, and perhaps how frustrated, she must have been, never to observe an egg in which this "male" developed, nor a hatching event!

We now know that the hectocotylus is only one of the arms of the male argonaut, an arm so greatly enlarged that it makes up nearly half his body. Into this arm he tucks packages of sperm, but no one has ever observed argonauts mating. We only know that at some point the hectocotylus detaches from the male and that he leaves it behind in the female's mantle, a hopeful love letter. He will never grow another hectocotylus and soon dies.

Though Cuvier's "worm" never existed, the word *hectocotylus* is now used for the specialized arms possessed by nearly all male cephalopods (although the hectocotyli of most species are not as enlarged and need not detach themselves to deliver sperm).

Jeanne sewed things up nicely with the argonaut. Although she didn't get all the answers, she investigated a plethora of open questions and painted a detailed picture of this unique shell maker. Argonauts are still the only animals we know that can grow and patch shells with their arms, as well as the only animals to evolve a new kind of shell long after their ancestral shells were lost. Jeanne had solved the mystery, and now she had only to tell the world about it.

Unfortunately, that would come with its own complications.

CHAPTER FIVE

THE
REPORTER

*Giovanna Power [is] a name well known among Italian and foreign scientists,
a name that evokes the study of the natural sciences. . . . Justice and truth
come together under the pen of the great Giovanna Power.*
—FRANCESCO ALDARESI, 1842

Although schools often teach "the scientific method" as a series of rote steps, science is and has always been a far more complex adventure. Some investigations call for formulating and testing hypotheses, as when Jeanne hypothesized that argonauts use their arms to make their shells. At other times, scientific work has no need of hypotheses, as when Jeanne recorded her observations of caterpillar grass preferences or sea star hunting habits. Experiments may provide answers, such as proving that snails can regrow their heads, or they may only open more questions, such as argonaut eggs that won't develop in isolation. (How do argonaut mothers keep their eggs alive? What precise environment does an argonaut egg need?)

But no matter how messy, creative, or unconventional, all scientific endeavors must include this crucial step: reporting.

To move discovery forward, scientists must share their observations, experimental methods, and results—whether or not the question was answered or the hypothesis was right. If science is not shared, future investigators are condemned to tackle issues that have already been resolved and hypotheses that have already been tested. If it is shared, then each generation can ask new questions based on the old discoveries.

FRIENDS AND SOCIETIES

In Jeanne's time as well as today, scientists often began the reporting process informally. They discussed their work with friends and colleagues, talking through their results and bouncing ideas off one another. Jeanne conversed with numerous Italian naturalists, notably the elder zoologist Carmelo Maravigna, who in his seventies was an established mentor in the Sicilian scientific community, and Anastasio Cocco, the young doctor who had observed the regeneration of Jeanne's triton snail.

Johannes Müller, who may have met Jeanne in Messina, studied everything from nerves, blood, and tumors to reptiles, insects, and sea urchins.

Messina also hosted frequent "tourists in science" from the rest of Europe. Among those who came to study on the island, Jeanne may have met Johannes Müller, a German scientist whose approach was "founded on a severe philosophical observation of nature." He and Jeanne would probably have bonded over their shared love for observable, recordable facts. Müller produced a definitive textbook on human anatomy, and he was also fascinated by reptiles, fish, and invertebrates. During his time in Messina, he might have called on Signora Power, delighting in her pet tortoise and her aquariums full of starfish and snails.

Jeanne surely discussed her discoveries with both visiting tourists and fellow residents. For the formal reporting step, however, she had to write a paper and submit it for presentation at a scientific society. The first such society was the Royal Society of London, founded in 1663, and the late eighteenth and nineteenth centuries brought a blossoming of scientific societies throughout Europe. London's Linnean Society was the first dedicated exclusively to biology. It was named after the prolific taxonomist Carl Linnaeus and founded in 1788, six years before Jeanne's birth. Some of the most influential ideas of the nineteenth century would be presented at meetings of the Linnean Society, including Charles Darwin's and Alfred Wallace's theory of evolution by natural selection.

At the societies' inception and for many years after, membership was limited to men. Specifically, white men. Linnaeus, who had classified and named not only *Argonauta argo* but also more than twelve thousand other living organisms, had taken the remarkably progressive step of grouping humans with other primates. He had also taken the horribly racist step of subdividing humans into "varieties" that associated derogatory features with skin color, describing the "Asiaticus" variety as "greedy" and the "Africanus" variety as "sluggish." This was a major contribution to the scientific racism that characterized Europe and America in the nineteenth century, when many influential white scientists argued that people of European descent were superior to all others.

As the Black writer and abolitionist Frederick Douglass pointed out in 1854, "Scientific writers, not less than others, write to please, as well as to instruct, and even unconsciously to themselves, (sometimes), sacrifice what is true to what is popular."

Eventually some societies began to admit members of excluded groups. The Linnean Society elected two Indian fellows in the 1860s and eventually eleven women in 1904. The Royal Society didn't admit its first female members until 1945,

This 1906 painting commemorates the Linnean Society's first female fellows signing the membership book and taking the hand of fellowship from the president. This group of eminent women did not include the one who had spearheaded the campaign for admission: botanist Marian Farquharson, whom the society obstinately refused to admit until 1908.

although a Moroccan ambassador had been admitted all the way back in 1682. Today, scientific societies around the world emphasize nondiscrimination in membership, and more and more of them are working to combat the systemic gender and racial inequity that inhibits so many potential scientists from obtaining the support of their peers. Jeanne was fortunate to find such support during her life.

The owl, laurel wreath, and Greek sigma in the Gioenia Academy's logo were drawn from old Catanian coins, and their motto "prudens magis quam loquax" means "wise rather than talkative"—a somewhat amusing choice for a society dedicated to talking about science.

For the first publication of her argonaut research, she did not write directly to the Linnean Society but began closer to home, with the Gioenia Academy in Catania, Sicily. In 1834 Maravigna read her paper to the assembled scientists during a meeting. (Only members could attend meetings, so it was fairly common for nonmembers to have their work read by a member.) Meticulous as always, Jeanne had provided him with physical shells and her own drawings, as well as written descriptions of her discoveries. The audience was intrigued but also skeptical. They suggested that Jeanne conduct further experiments, a common response of established scientists to new work by an unknown researcher.

She did and sent more results the following year. Satisfied and impressed, the members brought Jeanne into the fold as the first female member of the Gioenia Academy. They also encouraged her to publicize her results more broadly.

BETRAYAL IN PARIS

Jeanne was blessed with plenty of connections to help disseminate her research. Her merchant husband counted many friends among influential ship captains. One of these, a Commander Alban de Gasquet, visited James and Jeanne during a Messina port call in 1835. He may have met Mignonne the turtle or encountered the two lively martens who shared the Power home. Over dinner, perhaps, or after-dinner drinks, Jeanne told de Gasquet about her work with argonauts and its reception at the Gioenia Academy. The commander suggested that Jeanne send her results to Paris, a hotbed of scientific activity despite the on-again, off-again wars between the French and the English.

THE NAMING OF HUMANS

The woman who had been given the name Jeanne at birth, but was always called Lili by her family, published her scientific papers under the name Jeannette—a diminutive of Jeanne. Her preference for this name may have been personal, although some biographers speculate that she used it to avoid legal confusion over the fact that "Jeanne" had been declared dead as a child. The name Giovanna even shows up in some publications, a translation of Jeanne into Italian that reflects how thoroughly she had adopted Sicily as her home.

However, Jeanne stayed close to her French origins and continued to use her maiden name, Villepreux, in addition to her married name, Power, throughout her life. In modern writing about her, these two names are usually joined with a hyphen to make Villepreux-Power, matching the modern hyphenated style of combining last names.

Using both maiden and married names was far from common practice back when women were legally subsumed into their husband's family and household. But it's no surprise that Jeanne would do it, considering her strong-willed habit of bucking any trend she didn't care to conform to. She usually signed her papers, "Jeannette Power, née Villepreux," meaning "born Villepreux," and on later publications, "née de Villepreux."

That little article de—meaning "of"—is an interesting addition. It's called a nobiliary particle, similar to "von" in German surnames, and it's strongly associated with French nobility. But that doesn't mean every noble had a de in their name, or that every person with a de was noble. In the old days of the French monarchy, some families added the particle to their names just because they wanted to, and nobody stopped them. Then, during the French Revolution, nobility became extremely unpopular, and more than one family scratched out the particle in fear of the guillotine.

Was Jeanne born into a noble family? It's unclear, but certainly during her youth, nobody in her family used the nobiliary particle. Historians puzzled over the uncertain ancestry of the Villepreux family until 2022. As I was revising this book, the president of the Jeanne Villepreux-Power Association sent me the news that Jeanne's great-grandfather, Jean Nicolas de Villepreux, was the lieutenant of the Barony of Juillac. Had Jeanne done some genealogical research of her own, uncovered this connection, and adopted the nobiliary particle as a result? Perhaps. Another possibility is that she added the particle as a way of nodding to the status of her husband's family. The Power name has been associated with Irish nobility, although what relation James had to that part of the family is unclear.

Whatever the details, Jeanne obviously took pride in both her families, by birth and by marriage. I wonder if she would have wished for her aquatic inventions to be named Villepreux-Power cages?

De Gasquet told Jeanne that he had a friend in Paris, Sander Rang, who was a conchologist, a scientist who studies seashells. Since he would no doubt be fascinated by her work with argonaut shells, perhaps Rang could read her paper to the prestigious French Academy of Sciences, in the company of the great Cuvier. So Jeanne wrote a letter to Monsieur Rang and gave it to de Gasquet, along with her scientific report. The commander promptly delivered both letter and report to Rang, presumably in good faith that he had connected two biologists who would enjoy each other's work.

Rang never wrote back. As Jeanne later explained, "Having received no answer from M. Rang, although a long time had elapsed, I wrote him again; he kept a stubborn silence." He apparently had found her research a little *too* interesting and decided to pretend that he had conducted it himself. He embellished her paper with additional, falsified data. Perhaps he did this in order to justify putting his name on it or perhaps simply because he felt like it. He presented it all together as his own work, in 1837.

Jeanne found out what had transpired during a visit to London in April of that year. She was outraged. Not only had Rang stolen her discovery, but he had dared to add misinformation! His drawings of argonauts were inaccurate, and his claims about their behavior and reproduction incorrect. Given Jeanne's drive to uncover truth and challenge assumption, the factual errors probably galled her as much as the theft itself.

Luckily, Jeanne already had a proven track record of her accomplishments. The presentation of her work in Catania had been recorded in writing, and Maravigna had continued to be vocal in his support. She had published further reports with the Gioenia Academy in 1835 and 1836. In 1837 another professor, Scigliani, wrote about Jeanne's discovery for a general audience in the *Passatempo per le Dame*. That year, even as Jeanne must have been gnashing her teeth over Rang's betrayal, the Zoological Society of London recognized her accomplishment in designing underwater cages for the observation of marine animals by officially naming them Power cages.

Eventually, Jeanne wrote an addendum to her argonaut paper describing the debacle with Rang. Although there's no record that he suffered any professional consequences, everyone now accepted Jeanne's precedence in publishing her argonaut findings.

DENIAL AND DISASTER

Jeanne also had to contend with scientists who simply refused to believe her results. The most vociferous of these critics was the naturalist Henri de Blainville, who was certain that argonauts could never make their own shells.

Like Jeanne, Blainville had been born in the French countryside and moved to Paris in his youth, and also like Jeanne, he hadn't grown up with a passion for science but took up natural history as he discovered his proclivities. He studied in Paris under Cuvier, who helped him get a job as a professor. But the two didn't remain on good terms—Blainville, it seems, was not easy to get along with. He stayed in Paris for the rest of his career, eventually taking over Cuvier's job at the French Academy of Sciences after his mentor's death, and his research focused primarily on reptiles. Blainville, best remembered today for coining the word *paleontology*, made some forays into marine biology (he described a species of beaked whale that is known today as Blainville's beaked whale). But he worked in the old style, studying dead and dusty specimens. He knew his whale only from a jawbone he'd found in the museum.

Henri de Blainville criticized plenty of scientific ideas in addition to Jeanne's. He objected to early theories of evolution, although, had he lived long enough to read it, Darwin's presentation of natural selection might have changed his mind.

Hermit crabs evolved soft, curled abdomens that fit perfectly into snail shells and are immensely vulnerable without them. They depend not only on the snails who make the shells but also the snail-eating predators who create empty shells, as hermit crabs themselves do not eat snails.

Like many prominent scientists of his time (and let's be honest, plenty of people today), Blainville had a habit of forming strong opinions and holding onto them even in the face of contrary facts. According to his theory of biology, similarity in shape determined whether things were related to each other, so the difference in shape between an argonaut and her shell made it impossible that one could create the other. In 1837 he published a lengthy rebuttal of the evidence, insisting "that the animal found in the Argonaut is a parasite, inhabiting, like the Pagurus [hermit crab], a shell which does not belong to it." This was a direct response to Rang's publication, and although Blainville, to his credit, mentioned Jeanne's experiments as precursors to those of Rang, he then, much to his discredit, dismissed her work entirely and focused the rest of his paper on Rang. He even included a list of questions that he would like Rang to pursue, inasmuch as he was able—completely disregarding the fact that Jeanne had already pursued and answered these questions.

Some of Blainville's complaints may have resulted from genuine confusion, as it seems he was unable to access Jeanne's original papers and could read only Maravigna's abbreviated account of her research. Even so, his arguments verge on the absurd. If Jeanne's experiments were correct, then his theory of similarity in biology was flawed, and he fiercely resisted that possibility. He latched onto the fact that argonauts hatch without a shell and harped on it as proof conclusive that they are never able to make a shell, ignoring Jeanne's discovery that they begin to do so immediately after hatching. He insisted that the argonaut's mending of its shell must be done in an entirely different manner than the construction of a shell, and therefore has no relevance.

To hear Blainville not only contradict her results but also focus his attention on Rang's report must have infuriated Jeanne. On top of these frustrations, the greatest disappointment of all came the next year, when Jeanne was forty-three years old. She and James had moved from Messina to London at the end of 1837, for unspecified reasons, although we know they both had professional and personal connections in London. They traveled over land, and to lighten their luggage, they packed many belongings to send by sea, including Jeanne's invaluable natural treasures that she had collected, preserved, and recorded over her years in Sicily. In early 1838, sixteen cases of her possessions embarked for London on the brigantine *Bramley*.

Brigantines, a popular type of two-masted vessel, had been sailing—and wrecking—all around Europe for hundreds of years, as illustrated in this painting from around 1700.

The route from Sicily to England is rough in the winter, with frequent storms. The ship was wrecked, and the seafloor claimed Jeanne's collection, considered "among the richest and most singular of Europe."

FISH FRIENDS AND FISHY FRIENDS

In the midst of these struggles, Jeanne found solace in a network of friends who appreciated her intelligence, her wit and whimsy, and her indomitable spirit. Anastasio Cocco remained her staunch supporter. He worked as a pharmacist, mixing medicines as well as treating patients, and it's possible that his friendship and expertise had helped Jeanne develop her own secret elixir for preserving specimens. His other interests lay in the sea, but unlike Jeanne with her passion for mollusks, he was more drawn to fish. He would later have a fish named after him, *Microichthys coccoi*. And he himself honored Jeanne by naming a deep-sea fish from the Strait of Messina after her, *Gonostomus poweriae*.

Jeanne also cultivated a friendship with one of the most influential scientists of her day: the famous, and famously unpleasant, Richard Owen. Owen was an English geologist who coined the word *dinosaur* to describe the enormous fossil discoveries unearthed by Mary Anning and others. He was brilliant and vengeful—he used his influence to destroy the careers of anyone who disagreed with him, and he was known for his difficult personality.

Richard Owen poses with a crocodile skull in 1856. The complexity of his character encompasses brilliant scientific insight and plagiarism, vindictive vendettas and passionate public service.

However, like all humans, he was complicated. Even the worst person may occasionally do good, and Owen, for all his faults, was not the worst person. He and his wife became friends of the Powers, and Jeanne corresponded with him for years, sharing her papers and specimens. He supported her work publicly at London's prestigious Royal Society.

How Jeanne Villepreux-Power met Richard Owen is an intriguing question. It's possible that he was a friend of her husband's, as both had fathers who traded in the West Indies (ah, colonialism and the old boys' network). It's also possible that Jeanne, no slouch in putting herself forward, wrote him directly to introduce her work. Owen, having studied under Cuvier in Paris, spoke fluent French, so the two families could communicate in Jeanne's first language. Although she had been born in a rural town far from the hallowed halls of higher education, Jeanne was lucky to speak a literal *lingua franca*.

Caroline Owen, like the wives of many illustrious scientists so often neglected by history books, was an illustrious scientist in her own right. She kept up with the discoveries of the time, contributed to her husband's research, and wrote frequently about science in her diary. Here are her accounts of meeting with Jeanne in 1839, in which she refers to her husband as R., for Richard:

> **January 12th. We examined some of the eggs of the argonaut in the microscope. It was astonishing to see the tiny eggs containing the creature with its arms and immense eyes and the body like a cloud. There was no appearance of the rudimentary shell, but all seems to make it certain that it inhabits its own shell and no other. Mr. Broderip [a lawyer, shell collector, and friend of the Owens] also had a look afterwards. R. showed him the specimen in the bottle, and seemed to think the point was practically settled.**

> **26th. R. and I to Great Ormond Street, where Madame Power showed us her boxes of fossil shells, &c., and some molluscs in bottles, and, above all, the argonaut shells with the fractures made by her in her experiments, beautifully filled up and mended: three specimens in different stages of reconstruction, the first filled up with a substance like the lining membrane of a boiled egg. This was done about ten minutes after the piece was cut away by Madame Power; the more perfect restorations had the corrugations formed to match the rest.**

The word *octopus* was not yet in common English usage, having been introduced somewhat recently by Linnaeus. The French-derived word *poulpe* was often preferred by English speakers, as it was here by Caroline Owen:

> February 2.—R. to Madame Power's and brought away three bottles full of argonauts. A beautiful collection! One of them has the sail spread back over the shell, the suckers on the points [ridges of the shell]. Madame P. says that if we count the suckers they will be found to correspond with the number of points. This, with other circumstances, makes the question, I think, not whether the poulpe belongs to the shell, but how it has come to pass that, after so many have debated on the subject, Madame P has been the first to discover these things.

The respectful and admiring tone of Caroline Owen's diary contrasts with this letter written by Richard Owen after a later visit from Jeanne, in which his self-important and irascible personality shines through:

> Just as I had commenced my first cup, solacing myself with a chapter on German poets, Mrs. Wright, in answer to a bell, entered with a gloomy, awe-struck expression, announcing in a whisper—a Frenchwoman! So I had Madame Power instead of Goethe, and heard again the whole history of Argonauts and all the concomitant misfortunes, to which I submitted with great patience, finishing in the intervals of explanations my herring and toast.

A PERSISTENT PEN

Jeanne had spent her time in Sicily tramping over the island, gathering and collecting, counting and drawing. She had invented aquariums, designed experiments, and tested hypotheses. With all the material she had collected and planned to have with her in England, she probably expected to spend years—perhaps the rest of her life—writing up results, drawing fossils and specimens, and finding homes for them in museums and academies.

The shipwreck, sadly, sank these plans.

THE NAMING OF ANIMALS

Would you like to have a deep-sea fish named after you, as Jeanne did? Did you know that there's a horsefly named after Beyoncé? Who gives plants and animals their scientific names, and do these people follow rules, or do they pick any old name they want?

As it turns out, there are a lot of rules but also a lot of freedom. Scientific names are always Latinized, meaning that they follow the rules of Latin grammar, but they do not have to be real Latin words, or words in any language at all. Every organism has two names: first, the *genus*, which it shares with other closely related organisms, and second, the *species*, which is unique. An animal can't be given a name that already belongs to another animal—although it's possible for an animal and a plant to share a scientific name, as do *Orestias elegans*, the fish, and *Orestias elegans*, the orchid.

When a species first receives its scientific name, the name must be published, along with a thorough description of the organism. A *type specimen* (a dead and preserved individual of the species) must also be deposited in a publicly accessible location, usually a university or a museum, where other scientists can look at it.

One of the most well-known rules of naming species is that you're not supposed to name anything after yourself—only after somebody else. Naming species after one's collaborators, funding sources, family members, and friends are time-honored traditions. Naming species after famous figures, as in the case of *Scaptia beyonceae*, the horsefly with a bright golden rear end, is also an ancient practice.

The fish that bears Jeanne's name is a lightfish, smaller than a finger and dark in color, but glowing with rows of luminous photophores. Like many deep-sea animals, these lightfish come near the surface in the Strait of Messina, where Cocco discovered them. He named the species *Gonostomus poweriae*. Later analysis of its photophores led scientists to decide that this species and several others really belonged in a new genus, which they named *Vinciguerria* in honor of Italian ichthyologist Decio Vinciguerra. Vinciguerra (the person, not the fish) was only a child when Jeanne died, but her influence rippled through his life. He bred freshwater fish in Rome and restocked Italy's lakes and rivers, and when a Roman Aquarium was built in the 1880s, part of a wave of public aquariums opening in the second half of the century, he became its director.

The common name of *Vinciguerria poweriae* (stretching the definition of "common," as these fish are not exactly a frequent topic of conversation) is "Power's deep-water bristle-mouth fish." In print this name is already longer than the fish itself, so, honestly, why not make it a little longer still? See how "Villepreux-Power's deep-water bristle-mouth fish" rolls off the tongue!

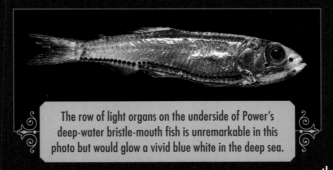

The row of light organs on the underside of Power's deep-water bristle-mouth fish is unremarkable in this photo but would glow a vivid blue white in the deep sea.

However, Jeanne had the opportunity to return to Messina for several shorter visits, the first almost immediately after the wreck. As she wrote from Sicily in February 1838, "The cause of my return was a serious illness of my husband, for the recovery of which the doctors of London found no other remedy than to return to Sicily. In truth I was very afraid of starting from here in late autumn [of 1837] that it would not be easy for him to withstand the rigors of the winter that came, and so it was; it is therefore convenient to wait here for his recovery (he is already in good condition) and then make a move again for England."

Jeanne made the most of this time, repeating her argonaut experiments and preserving a new series of argonaut shells in various stages of repair. She successfully brought these back to London, and they became the proof that she showed to the Owens, and that Richard subsequently presented to the Zoological Society. In 1839 she became a corresponding member, a type of membership for researchers living far from the society's headquarters, whose research was presented "by correspondence" rather than in person. In 1840 she received the gratifying news that Blainville had finally stopped opposing her argonaut results and published his acceptance that argonauts are not "parasites." In this, Blainville accomplished something that Richard Owen was never able to do in his career: change his mind and admit publicly that he had been wrong.

Jeanne may have illustrated the frontispiece to her *Guida per la Sicilia* herself. An argonaut shell is its central feature, surrounded by a combination of human-built and nature-grown wonders.

Jeanne's return visits to Sicily in 1838 and 1839 also allowed her to complete a detailed guidebook to the island, including at least one map she drew herself. She covered Sicily's history, geography, art and culture and, of course, its natural history. What had first been published in an incomplete form in 1839 as *Itinerario della Sicilia* became Jeanne's exhaustive *Guida per la Sicilia* in 1842. It retained enough general interest to be reprinted in 1995 and again in 2008.

Jeanne continued to travel between France, Italy, and England for the rest of her life. She kept in touch with her family in Juillac, likely visiting when her

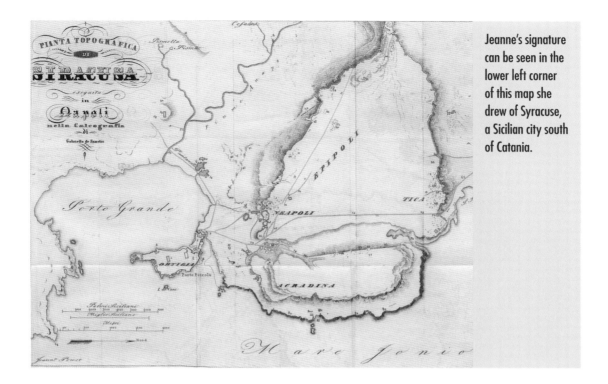

Jeanne's signature can be seen in the lower left corner of this map she drew of Syracuse, a Sicilian city south of Catania.

father died in 1840. Her younger brother Joseph still lived there; he had been only two years old when their mother died and had never learned to read and write. Jeanne had probably been more of a mother than a sister to him when she lived at home, and her care extended into their adult lives. In 1844 she gave him her family inheritance, and the following year she bought land in Juillac for him to use. He had married and, like Jeanne, had no children. As for Jeanne's surviving sister, Marie, she probably got married too and perhaps moved away from Juillac, since she wasn't included in the sibling property share. If not as rich as Jeanne, she at least seems to have been well enough provided for that her older sister didn't feel the need to step in.

Later in life, Jeanne discovered that a few of her research notes had not been lost in the shipwreck after all. "In the confusion of packing-up, preparatory to my departure from Sicily, my manuscripts were mislaid, and I have only just discovered them amongst some old papers; I therefore hasten to lay the following observations before you." Jeanne wrote these words to preface an 1857 article that contained all her studies on animals other than argonauts: the common octopuses, the starfish and snails, the martens, and tortoise. What good fortune for Jeanne—and now for us—to have these studies resurface!

Jeanne's only surviving scientific illustration features an argonaut shell so exquisitely rendered it almost looks like a photograph. The composition embodies Jeanne's thinking that an animal is best known and studied in its natural environment.

Though nearly all her art either sank with the ship or was lost to time, we do have an exquisite painting of an argonaut that Jeanne completed in 1839. In this piece, she captured the delicate curve and ripples of the shell, the impressive and slender length of the octopus's arms. She placed the animal in a complex habitat of coral and barnacles, and with the subtle use of color made everything appear to be viewed through water.

Jeanne and James both lived long enough for photographic portraits to have become practical and popular. In 1861 they had their portraits taken by the famous French photographer André-Adolphe-Eugène Disdéri, who a few years earlier had patented his system of printing photographs as small paper *cartes de visite*, or "visiting cards." Members of the upper class used these like business cards, writing their addresses or other notes on the back and exchanging them at meetings and social calls. This portrait remains the only known photograph of Jeanne ever taken.

CONTINUED CURIOSITY

Jeanne published her final paper in 1867, a few years before her death. "Observations on the Origin of Meteorites, Aeroliths, Bolides, or Stones That Are Said to Have Fallen from the Sky" was Jeanne's only foray into meteorology. She'd heard of an 1803 meteorite shower in the town of L'Aigle, France, and she knew that the scientist who'd studied it, Jean-Baptiste Biot, had concluded the meteorites were extraterrestrial in origin. But she was skeptical. It is quite an absurd idea (albeit true) that a large quantity of stones could fall to Earth from outer space, and Jeanne thought she had a more prosaic explanation.

She had seen waterspouts and tornadoes in Sicily pick up sand, water, and, most important, rocks. What simpler reason could there be for the fall of stones from the air than that they had been picked up by a tornado and dropped in some other location? She did have to account for the high iron content of meteorites, and her agile mind produced this possibility: "Waterspouts would have picked up iron or iron-bearing sand, which is found in several points on the globe, melted it, agglomerated it, then thrown it to the ground."

She was completely wrong. Waterspouts and tornadoes can pick up stones, but they cannot melt or transform them into meteorites. Biot had ascertained correctly that meteorites come from space, and by continuing to research these "aeroliths" (an old-fashioned name that comes from the Greek words for "air" and "stone"), scientists have learned in detail the chemicals that make up our solar system.

However, I find Jeanne's meteorite paper fascinating. For one thing, it's a welcome reminder that scientists both famous and obscure can make mistakes in their arguments and errors in their logic. For another, it shows that Jeanne was never afraid to question accepted explanations. Instead of believing everything she read, she drew conclusions from her own experience. That doesn't mean her conclusions were always right, but it is why she could contribute so significantly to science. She didn't shy away from astronomy because it was new to her, nor did she keep her thoughts to herself to avoid ridicule. She plunged right in and gave it her best try—which is really all that any of us can do.

CHAPTER SIX

THE
LUMINARY

I am amazed to see so much sagacity, patience and unexpected results of observations and discoveries. . . . These discoveries have been fruitful of other discoveries, and who knows how many other discoveries in the future.
—CARMELO MARAVIGNA, WRITING ABOUT JEANNE'S RESEARCH IN 1836

Jeanne's work was instrumental in creating the modern field of marine biology. When she began her research, aquatic animals were studied almost exclusively from land—by catching them, killing them, dissecting them, and drawing and preserving the bodies. There was no scuba diving, no submarines or submersibles, not even a camera that could take pictures underwater.

But Jeanne had the imagination to conceive of aquariums and the perseverance to see her idea through. The acumen and creativity with which she designed and executed replicable tests for her ideas were harbingers of a new science. Her artistic skills, which she used to document her discoveries, and her determination to promote her work and get credit for it, were nearly as important.

She was not alone in pushing this sea change. Many people in many countries were working to advance the study of animals in their natural habitat, alongside predators and prey. When it came to visualizing underwater life, a remarkable development came from an unexpected source: a painting created primarily to make money, with science as an afterthought.

LINKING PAST AND FUTURE, EARTH AND SEA

The painting is called *Duria Antiquior, a More Ancient Dorset*. It was groundbreaking in two ways. First, it was the earliest example of what is now called paleoart: artistic reconstruction, based on fossils, of what extinct animals might have looked like and how they might have behaved. Second, as far as we know, *Duria Antiquior* was the first "split-screen" illustration. It shows life underwater and above water as one connected ecosystem (although the word *ecosystem* wouldn't be coined until a hundred years later).

Duria Antiquior, a More Ancient Dorset is a fascinating work of art—part educational diagram, part stylized cartoon, and part money-making gambit.

It's likely that Jeanne saw *Duria Antiquior* at some point, since it was painted in 1830, in the midst of her aquarium development. The painter, English geologist Henry De la Beche, based the work largely on fossils found by Mary Anning. At the time, Anning was struggling financially. She relied on sales of fossils to the wealthy tourists who visited her seaside town of Lyme Regis, and an economic downturn in the 1820s cut into her income.

De la Beche, a friend and admirer of Anning's who also lived in Lyme, conceived of *Duria Antiquior* as a way to raise money for her—a nineteenth-century GoFundMe. He drew the original art and then had a London illustrator turn it into a lithograph that could be used to print multiple copies. De la Beche sold the prints and gave all the money to Anning.

Jeanne had visited England and corresponded with English scientists, and she may have heard of the print through them. Perhaps she even purchased a copy, one female scientist reaching out to support another. If she did see *Duria Antiquior*, she would certainly have made a close examination of its representation of cephalopods. At first glance, large toothy reptiles dominate the painting, but several squidlike creatures called belemnites can be seen underwater, as well as the coiled ammonites. Belemnites grew hard shells inside their bodies, rather than outside, and Anning collected these fossilized shells to sell alongside her ammonites. She even discovered belemnites with fossilized ink sacs, supporting their similarity to modern squid. Ammonites offered fewer clues as to what the animals inside the shells would have looked like or how they would have behaved.

Because some ammonite shells look similar to argonaut shells, a few people speculated that they might have looked and acted like argonauts. The resemblance between argonauts and some species of ammonites is so strong that as recently as 1996, a fringe scientist suggested that argonauts evolved directly from ammonites.

Ammonites like this Jurassic *Arietites* used their mantles to create coiled shells. Filling chambers in these shells with buoyant gas kept the animals from sinking to the seafloor.

(They didn't—ammonites went extinct at the same time as the dinosaurs, and the first argonauts didn't show up in the fossil record until tens of millions of years later.) To reconstruct a living ammonite with inspiration from argonauts was a reasonable concept in 1830, so De la Beche drew an ammonite "sailing" on the sea surface with two arms unfurled to catch the wind. You know, like argonauts do. Except they don't.

Jeanne was in the midst of proving that argonauts use their arm membranes to build their shells. However, even she was reluctant to discount the weight of so many years' authority and conviction, and at first referred to the argonaut's two unusual arms as "sailing arms," even writing in 1839, "as everyone knows, it is employed by the animal as a sail." By 1856 she would call them "membranous arms," and focus confidently on their function in creating and maintaining the shell.

Jeanne's work and De la Beche's would later be joined in harmony, when the term "aquarium view" was coined to describe the innovative style of split-level art that originated with *Duria Antiquior.*

THE AQUARIUM CRAZE

Thanks in part to Jeanne's pioneering work, a fascination with aquariums began to sweep across England, Germany, and the United States in the second half of the nineteenth century. People who never thought of themselves as any kind of scientist delighted in viewing ocean animals through glass windows.

Other innovators also contributed significantly to the development and spread of aquariums. One such early aquarist was Anna Thynne, who kept corals in her London home. Thynne, like Jeanne, was a lady of means. Her marriage to an English lord afforded her all the money and leisure she needed to pursue a life of science, and she had become particularly fascinated with corals on a trip to the seaside. They looked like rocks but lived like animals.

Thynne collected corals, sewed them onto sponges, and brought them home with a large quantity of seawater. She kept them in glass bowls and replaced their water regularly until she ran out of seawater, then switched to aerating the water by pouring it from one bowl to another. It was a lot of work, and Thynne was rich, so she delegated the task to a servant. *Better*, she must have thought, *but still not ideal.* How could she replicate the corals' natural environment so they could live without constant coddling?

People knew by then that plants and animals on land had a mutually beneficial arrangement. Thynne was probably familiar with Joseph Priestley's experiments nearly a hundred years earlier, in which he'd found that a rat sealed in a glass jar would breathe all the available oxygen and then die of suffocation, while the addition of a plant would keep the rat alive. She decided to try adding marine plants to the water with her corals. After a couple of years of experiments, her servants could finally take a break. By 1849 Thynne had created the first balanced marine aquarium—a self-contained ecosystem, with plants and animals exchanging oxygen and carbon dioxide through the water.

Anna Thynne accomplished a remarkable feat—even today, it's far easier to construct a self-sustaining aquarium with freshwater than salt water. Even with the living inhabitants of the aquarium in balance, her servants probably still had to replace water lost due to evaporation.

Jeanne had never attempted to create something like this, since she lived on the coast with a constant supply of seawater. While Thynne focused on keeping her corals alive far from the sea, Jeanne's attention had gone toward keeping her animals undisturbed so that she could observe their behavior. Both were major players in the history of marine biology, but neither coined the word *aquarium*.

That honor belongs to the naturalist Philip Henry Gosse, who invented *aquarium* by shortening the phrase "aquatic vivarium." Gosse created the first public aquarium at the London Zoo in 1853, and the "Fish House" was soon crowded with visitors. Once they saw it, the rich wanted to bring it into their own homes. It was at once a demonstration of chemical and biological principles, and an expensive decoration. Interest in private aquariums exploded, and fish tanks became a fad to follow cabinets of curiosity.

Jeanne was well aware of this growing popularity. She also must have realized that the idea did not belong to her alone. Humans have been sticking fish in bowls probably longer than we have recorded ourselves doing so. Goldfish were kept as pets in China hundreds if not thousands of years ago. However, Jeanne knew that she was the one who had designed structures to keep marine animals alive so their natural behaviors could be observed and documented, and she wanted everyone else to know it too.

She wrote to Richard Owen, "I have read in several newspapers that there is a lot of care for Aquaria or cages. You know, Sir, that from 1832 until 1842, I took care of it. I had invented several in 1832 and 1834, which I had placed in my house, as you know, for the study of the Argonaut and other marine animals, and other cages in the sea." She added, "Since I was the first to have the idea of studying marine animals in Aquaria or cages, I want to keep my inventor rights."

Owen, in a surprisingly gracious move, wrote in his article about mollusks for the eighth edition of the *Encyclopaedia Britannica* that Jeanne should be credited as the inventor of these marvelous new tools. The term *aquariophily* had arisen to describe the general passion for aquariums, and Owen dubbed Jeanne the Mother of Aquariophily. In the following edition, unfortunately, changes to the article removed Jeanne's credit.

Although her name is no longer associated with them, today aquariums are everywhere—in public institutions, private homes, restaurants, and dental offices. They are not, however, Jeanne's only long-lived legacy.

RIPPLES OF RESEARCH

A young Swiss scientist named Albert von Kölliker visited Messina when he was in his early twenties. He missed seeing Jeanne, as she and James had just left Sicily for London, but her research may have been a formative influence. Kölliker became fascinated by cephalopods, particularly their embryonic development, and he eventually published an iconic work on the topic.

Kölliker also wrote a paper in 1845 about the hectocotylus of argonauts and the hectocotylus of the related (but shell-less) octopus species *Tremoctopus*. In this paper, he expounded "the Hypothesis that these Hectocotylae are the Males of the Cephalopoda upon which they are found," giving Jeanne credit for coming up with the idea and adding details for *Tremoctopus*. In studying the hectocotyli, he was "unable to find organs

Albert von Kölliker was as interested in the microscopic structure of animals as he was in their macroscopic anatomy, which led him to discover mitochondria—the tiny energy factories inside our cells.

either of sight or hearing" and lamented that "notwithstanding repeated observations, I was not able to find an anal orifice." Nevertheless, he strongly endorsed Jeanne's case for the hectocotylus as the male of the species.

Discoveries proceeded fairly rapidly in the following years. The German scientist Heinrich Müller (not to be confused with an infamous Nazi war criminal who would share his name a century later) found small octopuses with an arm that would "drop off on being touched" and "resembled the *Hectocotylus Octopodis* of Cuvier." While in Messina and "very desirous of repeating the observations of Madame Power," he figured out that these small octopuses were adult male argonauts. In 1852 he published a paper identifying the hectocotylus as an arm of the male and describing the process of its detachment. He wrote, "The name 'Hectocotylus' may very well be retained, without any implication of independent animality." And so it was that even lacking "independent animality," the term *hectocotylus* even expanded to include, a few years later in 1857, the equivalent if nondetachable sperm-carrying arm in males of nearly all cephalopod species.

Although the "Sailing Cuttle Fish" description is inaccurate, this colored wood engraving from *The National Encyclopedia* showcases exquisite anatomical detail.

Meanwhile, although Jeanne's proof that the argonaut uses its arms to build its shell rather than to catch wind was accepted as conclusive by her scientific colleagues, the powerful image of an argonaut bobbing along at the surface with its "sails" out proved hard to shake. Perhaps if more of Jeanne's illustrations had survived to be printed and disseminated along with her words, things might have gone differently.

As it was, even *The National Encyclopedia* printed in London in the 1880s still described argonauts as "Sailing Cuttle Fish." And art clearly imitating the early drawings of argonaut sailors was printed in 1941, a full hundred years after Jeanne discredited it.

The topic of molluscan regeneration has remained evergreen, as both scientists and the general public are endlessly fascinated by the ability of certain animals to regrow body parts. In 2021 a sea slug, a relative of the garden snails that Spallanzani decapitated and the marine snails that Jeanne similarly mutilated, was discovered with the ability to separate its head from its body and regrow an entirely new body from the severed head. Jeanne would have been delighted! Scientists still haven't figured out how to imbue humans with superpowers on par with sea slugs, but they've made a huge step forward with the discovery of stem cells, which can divide to produce many kinds of cells, from brain and blood to bone and muscle. In fact, stem cell

A wood engraving from 1893 offers a fantastical representation of an argonaut using her shell as a boat and her arms as sails.

research has kicked off a whole new field called regenerative medicine.

FISH FARMS AND SEA LABS

Jeanne knew that many people are interested in marine animals for the primary purpose of eating them—after all, she got most of her scientific specimens from fishers. She herself was no vegetarian. Living in a wealthy household in Messina in the 1800s, her diet would have included plenty of meat and fish.

Jeanne looked at animals with a combination of empathy and dispassion. She felt affectionate toward those she brought into her home and admired and appreciated the ones she watched in the wild. At the same time, she was willing to hurt and kill animals to learn about them. She probably felt no qualms about using animals as food.

In addition to the concerns that many people raise today about using animals in laboratory research, some loudly voice objections to eating animals. Throughout history, the world's human population has been fed through the sacrifice of countless animal lives. Is it possible to weigh a farm animal's pain against a lab animal's? If we are disturbed by the thought of a scientist like Jeanne cutting off an octopus's arm to see if it can survive, ought we be more or less disturbed by an octopus fisher who pulls octopuses out of the water and lets them suffocate on the way to market? One creates knowledge, the other food.

Fishing faces an additional ethical dilemma. Many species have been driven extinct (such as sea cows) or been fished to the point of population collapse (such as bluefin tuna) by humanity's hunger. The word *overfishing* describes the capture of so many individual fish that the ones left can't reproduce quickly enough to replenish the population. And just because a species isn't technically a fish, like shrimp or clams, doesn't render it immune to overfishing.

In Jeanne's time, most people believed the ocean was so vast that humans could never affect it. Overfishing animals in the open sea, they thought, was impossible. However, they had seen it happen in smaller bodies of water, such as lakes and rivers, and they had seen nearshore oyster beds severely depleted through overharvest. Jeanne herself noted that "the rivers of Sicily contain very few fish, and crayfish are totally lacking." She promptly suggested that "we could repopulate these rivers, as well as the lakes."

This was a bold idea, born from Jeanne's years of exploration, tramping over Sicily to understand the island's natural history, as well as from her work with aquariums. She had realized that Power cages could be used to raise fish from eggs, protecting them from predators as they grew and making it easy to collect the adults. "When the small fish have reached the desired size," she wrote, "we would . . . transport them elsewhere."

Raising fish or other aquatic animals in submerged enclosures is called aquaculture, and it has been practiced since antiquity to produce seafood. It had become less common in France after the Revolution, and Jeanne's suggestion was part of a broader movement toward reviving and improving the old fish farms. Biologist Victor Coste had developed innovative techniques to grow oysters on tiles and trays, replenishing France's stocks of this precious edible animal. In 1859 he established a marine station in Concarneau, France—only the second such facility in the world, and the oldest still operating today. The facility's initial purpose was seafood production, but it quickly became a haven for many kinds of marine research, as well as a forerunner of marine laboratories around the world. Perhaps the most influential has been the Stazione Zoologica in Naples, Italy. It opened in

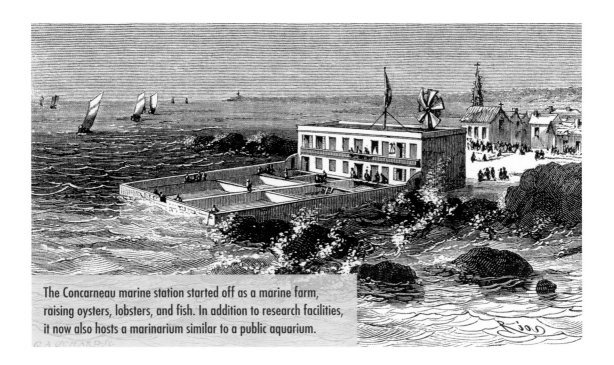

The Concarneau marine station started off as a marine farm, raising oysters, lobsters, and fish. In addition to research facilities, it now also hosts a marinarium similar to a public aquarium.

1874, just three years after Jeanne's death, and scientists flocked there to investigate the abundant marine life in and around the Strait of Messina, whose exploration Jeanne and her friend Cocco had pioneered. Meanwhile, the new wave of Italian aquaculture eventually led to Vinciguerra restocking the country's lakes and rivers with freshwater fish—just as Jeanne had suggested.

JEANNE'S LATER YEARS

The frequent travel undertaken by Jeanne and James from 1837 onward likely resulted from their diverse family and professional connections, especially as James shifted his career into new fields. By 1838 he had left his job as a merchant for a foray into industrial chemistry.

His company produced silver nitrate, which was critical in the early days of photography, and an important compound in medicine and biology. Before the age of antibiotics, which would begin in 1928 with the discovery of penicillin, silver nitrate was one of the most reliable antiseptics for preventing wounds from becoming infected. It also was and remains an effective stain, which can be annoying (if you're handling it without gloves) or useful (if you apply it to cells you'd like to view under a microscope, as it highlights shapes and structures that would otherwise be nearly invisible).

James, who seems to have been as much of an irrepressible polymath as his wife, branched out anew in the 1850s, when he began working on the first underwater telegraph lines. Since its invention in the 1830s, the telegraph had become the pinnacle of modern technology, the first *instant communication* precursor to phones and internet. James moved back and forth between the British Isles and continental Europe to ensure the success of the telegraph cables connecting the two.

Jeanne may well have taken an interest in James's various ventures, especially considering her own background in both chemistry (to preserve specimens) and engineering (to design dresses and aquariums). And James, for his part, might have been intrigued by Jeanne's ongoing experiments. But the couple defied a common pattern for marriages at the time by continuing to pursue their separate careers

At various times, James Power managed merchant ships, chemical production, and communications—an excellent match for the equally multifaceted Jeanne.

over the years. Unlike many women, such as Caroline Owen, Jeanne showed no inclination to join her husband as an assistant in his work. And unlike many men, James made not the slightest effort to take credit for his wife's remarkable research—not that Jeanne was likely to have permitted it.

In whatever country she found herself, Jeanne never stopped corresponding with scientific societies (she was a member of a dozen by now, all more open-minded about admitting women than the Linnean Society) and individual colleagues. However, she never again got out into nature to gather specimens and experiment the way she had done in Sicily.

One reason for Jeanne's shift from experimental activity to publishing may have been the geopolitical climate of the time. The latter half of her life was marked by the turmoil of revolution and war, just as her early years had been. Revolutions in 1830 and 1848 eventually led to a second French Empire, ruled by Napoleon III, nephew of the first Napoleon, who dreamed of rebuilding his uncle's dominion. The rest of Europe wasn't about to take that lying down, and the new Napoleon's most powerful opponent emerged in the form of a unified Germany, called the Prussian Empire. The resulting Franco-Prussian War led to an attack on Paris by the Prussian army in 1870.

The royal wedding that had connected Jeanne and James over fifty years earlier, although intended to promote peace in France and the surrounding countries, in reality did no such thing. The monarchy had returned to France, but the legacy of the Revolution and Napoleon remained.

Having arrived in Paris as a young woman in the midst of the Napoleonic Wars, as an old lady Jeanne barely managed to escape the city before it was besieged. While the Prussian soldiers marched toward Paris, she fled to her hometown of Juillac, where she could visit siblings, nieces, and nephews. James stayed behind, still working actively with the telegraph company. No doubt the two hoped to be reunited after the siege. After all, they had weathered half a century of political instability together.

But this time, their separation was permanent. Jeanne died in 1871, at the venerable age of seventy-six, leaving behind a tremendous scientific legacy. James followed less than a year later and was buried by her side in the Juillac cemetery.

UNCOVERING THE PAST

The story of Jeanne is inextricable from the story of her historians and biographers. Although she assiduously published her scientific results, she left very little writing about other aspects of her life. Furthermore, much of her professional work lies at the bottom of the sea. The details of the construction of her first aquarium are as murky as the details of her long walk to Paris.

This small mausoleum in the Juillac cemetery once housed the bodies of both Jeanne and James. When the cemetery was destroyed, they were reburied in unmarked graves.

In the years immediately following Jeanne's death, memory of her accomplishments faded. She left no children who might have championed her story, and the conflict throughout Europe—in France especially—distracted from scientific and historical pursuits. Revolution was followed by revolution, one world war by another.

However, Jeanne's life and research have always captured the interest of those who rediscover them. Within a few decades of her death, two provincial French newspapers published articles about her life, probably based on interviews with people who had known her at least a little. These brief biographies themselves contain no references or named authorities, so we cannot be certain of their accuracy. Still, they have become the basis for everything subsequently written about Jeanne.

These early authors were entranced by the "fairy-tale" aspect of Jeanne's story. They compared her to the princess in the popular French story *Donkeyskin*, who endured hardships early in life and was eventually swept off to her happily-ever-after life by a prince (Jeanne's "prince," of course, was James Power). Thankfully, these accounts did not end the story there but used it as a springboard to write admiringly of Jeanne's dedication to science and the importance of her discoveries.

But in emphasizing the romantic nature of the story, it's possible that these authors exaggerated or even invented details. Accounts differ on the Villepreux family's financial situation. Sometimes they are described as very poor, requiring Jeanne to work outside the home from an early age. But historical details unearthed later indicate they were well off, with a house in the village square.

Then, because heartbreak builds more sympathy for the heroine, some versions have her loving a boy in Juillac whose family disapproved. Her opaque comment to the mayor that "you know what my position was, and the reasons for my departure" invites wild speculation but confirms nothing! As for the difficulty with her cousin en route to Paris, we may never know exactly what happened, only that Jeanne parted ways with him and ended up stuck with the authorities of Orléans.

The dramatic appeal of Jeanne's story is so powerful that in 2009 a well-known French author, Claude Duneton, wrote a fictionalized biography called *La Dame de l'Argonaute* (The Lady of the Argonaut). He invented dialogue and intimate inner thoughts to fill Jeanne's early life, her trip to Paris, and her meeting with James. It isn't factual, but it's a compelling read, evidence of the strength of the twenty-first-century revival of interest in Jeanne.

A RISING TIDE OF INTEREST

"Each twenty years she is rediscovered," says French historian of science Josquin Debaz, who has dug deep into the writing by and about Jeanne. "Sometimes it's more of a fairy tale biography, sometimes it's more the fact that she was a woman scientist."

Her modern rediscovery and its still-growing momentum were sparked by the enthusiasm of biologist Claude Arnal. Although he was born in Juillac, he learned about Jeanne only when he retired to his hometown at the end of his scientific career. Fascinated by her life and surprised by its obscurity, he brought his research skills to bear and began tracking down original papers, letters, and documentation.

In the early 1990s, Arnal's careful mapping of Jeanne's life coincided with an entirely different kind of mapping project—the Magellan probe's mission to Venus. Magellan discovered hundreds of new craters, and NASA invited the public to propose names for them. As a press release explained, "Many features on Venus, by international agreement, are named for goddesses of ancient religions and cultures. But craters and volcanic calderas or vents, the paterae, are named for actual women . . . [who] must have been deceased for at least three years, and must have been in some way notable or worthy of the honor."

Jeanne had been deceased, at this point, for 120 years, and Arnal considered her notability beyond dispute. He wrote to the Magellan Project proposing her name, and while that process rolled slowly forward, he published a short biography of Jeanne in the Bulletin of The Malacological Society of London. He also wrote to the Messina History Society, and Michela d'Angelo, a professor who studies the history of foreigners in Messina, wrote back. As she says, "I thought that Messina, the town where the Powers resided for 25 years,

Venus, the only planet in the solar system named for a female rather than a male goddess (unless you're inclined to refer to Earth as Gaia), has been given a naming convention to honor other female figures from myth and history.

should do something to remember them. What better than the reprint of her second book, *Guida per la Sicilia*?" So she made it happen in 1995.

In 1997 Arnal's proposal was accepted, and Jeanne's name was given to a Venusian patera, an irregularly shaped crater usually formed by volcanoes. It was Jeanne's first namesake to use both her preferred surnames: the Villepreux-Power Patera. (Happily, there is also an Anning Patera for Mary Anning.)

Arnal continued to campaign for Jeanne's recognition, and in 2005 he shared her story with artist Anne-Lan who was organizing an arts and sciences event for Limousin, the region of France where Juillac is located. Anne-Lan decided that Jeanne would be the perfect figurehead for the event. She went on to help Arnal found the Jeanne Villepreux-Power Association in 2008, in which Arnal remained active until his death in 2020—while I was in the midst of working on this book.

The house where Jeanne lived, along with most of the city of Messina, was destroyed by a terrible earthquake in 1908. Artist Anne-Lan re-created what it might have looked like, filling the canvas with meaningful objects—such as a statue of Venus to represent the Villepreux-Power Patera.

Anne-Lan wrote of Arnal, "He will be greatly missed because all our work was the extension of his own desire, to do justice to a wonderful forgotten woman . . . when we look at Venus in the starry sky, we will have affectionate thoughts for them both."

Anne-Lan has carried on Arnal's promotional work and even convinced the mayor of Paris to name one of the paths in the city's largest park Allée Jeanne Villepreux-Power. She also painted a richly detailed canvas of Jeanne at work in her home laboratory. The marine biologist wears a gown reminiscent of the *chemise à la reine* as she shares her chair with a pine marten. The other marten prowls across a table covered with books, seashells, and Greek sculpture, while the port of Messina is displayed through a wide window. On the wall beside the window hangs Jeanne's own painting of the argonaut, and a glass aquarium is just visible behind a curtain. D'Angelo, too, continues to advance Jeanne's memory, with the project of naming the Messina city aquarium after her.

As word of Jeanne and her accomplishments spreads, so does her creative inspiration. Musician Timothy Sellers recorded a song about Jeanne in 2008 for the V track of his alphabetical album *26 Scientists*. Berlin gallery STATE Studio dedicated the art exhibition Power Cage to Jeanne in 2019. These diverse works are the perfect homage to a scientist whose originality shone through every aspect of her life.

"The spectrum of her abilities is very wide," says Debaz. "She domesticates the marten and observes its behavior. She knows how to draw topographical maps and paints her specimens in superb watercolors . . . she publishes about butterflies, or later about meteors. In addition, she perfected original conservation procedures which would enable some of her collections to serve in London as tangible proof, to be opposed to the dry and rigid shells of her opponents. And even more, to carry out her long-term observations and experiments, she invents and develops the first modern forms of the aquarium."

Jeanne may be most famous for her invention of aquariums, but it's important to remember *why* she invented them. She wanted to study marine animals—especially argonauts—in captivity. This had never been done before. "I think the most important part is that she was experimenting," Debaz says. "Because at that time, in zoology, it wasn't very common. She was very advanced for her time."

Jeanne's struggles against sexism probably helped inspire her experimentalism. Established male scientists could publish opinions on natural history from their drawing rooms, but Jeanne lacked that "legitimacy." Debaz says, "She had to grab this power of experimentation to confront them, because she was a woman and [they thought] she cannot be trusted."

Jeanne's fierce determination to not only discover the answers to her questions but to be believed by her colleagues led her to inventions both physical and intellectual. Her engagement with the scientific community is as much a part of her legacy as her experiments with argonauts. Jeanne's story reminds us that science, and science history, is created not merely by individual scientists but by their interactions with one another—and with the broader world around them.

MARINE BIOLOGY TODAY AND TOMORROW

*My unexpected departure from Messina forced me to suspend the work I loved.
I desire with all my heart that these studies be continued by some patient
naturalist; I say patient, that's the word, because you must be extremely so.*
—JEANNE VILLEPREUX-POWER

Jeanne gave the world a clear view of one of the strangest and most marvelous ocean animals: the argonaut octopus. Her observations began the process of experimental inquiry into their lives and habits, an inquiry that continues to reveal surprising secrets.

Some ocean animals are mysterious because they live far from shore or deep below sunlit water. Argonauts are in neither category. They have lived alongside humans for millennia, managing so far to survive fishing and shipping and oil spills and climate change, yet they maintain their mystery. Despite how long people have been familiar with argonauts, it wasn't until Jeanne's work two hundred years ago that we learned they make their own shells. And it wasn't until a mere decade ago that we learned how they use their shells.

For at least a hundred years, scientists had noticed bubbles inside argonaut shells, but no one knew why the bubbles were there. Some thought they were accidental acquisitions; others thought they must serve a purpose. It was reminiscent of the "shell stealer or shell maker?" debate. In 2010 two octopus scientists, Julian Finn and Mark Norman, answered the question in a way that would make Jeanne proud, by experimenting on argonauts in their own habitat. Instead of merely theorizing, the scientists donned their scuba gear and headed into the water where they carefully collected three argonauts. They "burped" the bubbles from their shells and then released them.

All three argonauts swam to the surface, opened their shells to get a new bubble, and sealed it in with their arms. Then they swam down to the precise depth at which the air in the bubble would keep them neutrally buoyant, neither floating nor sinking. Thus balanced for ideal swimming, the argonauts went about their business.

This remarkable discovery breathed new life into the old idea that argonauts use their shell as a boat. But instead of a sailboat, as Pliny suggested, it's more like a carefully pressurized submarine! How delighted Jeanne would be—and perhaps wistful that she hadn't been able to conduct such a beautifully straightforward experiment herself.

Finn has also worked to clarify the number of argonaut species. Because of the way argonauts make and mend their shells, with their arms instead of their mantle, their shell shape can be much more variable than in other mollusks. This variation has led scientists to name dozens of argonaut species based on shell differences, but Finn's close examination confirms that there are only four living species (and several more extinct ones, identified from fossils). In addition to the greater argonauts (*Argonauta argo*), which

This stunning photograph showcases the translucence of the argonaut's shell, which Jeanne found the animal could see through like a window.

Jeanne studied, today's oceans are home to the smaller muddy argonauts (*Argonauta hians*), knobby argonauts (*Argonauta nodosus*), and Noury's argonaut (*Argonauta nouryi*). The first two are found around the world, while knobby argonauts are restricted to the Southern Hemisphere and Noury's argonauts have been found only in the Pacific Ocean. We know almost nothing about the distinct habits of each species, since they are so rarely seen in the wild. And although we've developed considerable advancements in aquarium technology since Jeanne's inventions, argonauts still don't do well when separated from the sea in captivity.

Many other confounding aspects of argonaut behavior remain for an enterprising science student to tackle. In recent years, argonauts have often been sighted clinging to jellyfish in the open ocean, to the amusement of divers. A new fad? Or perhaps argonauts have done this for ages, but humans have only begun to observe it now that we're exploring the sea in record numbers.

The smallest argonauts seem to ride passively on jellyfish like little hitchhikers. As they grow to match or exceed the jellies' size, they seem to start dragging the jellies around. Perhaps they use the stinging tentacles as protection against

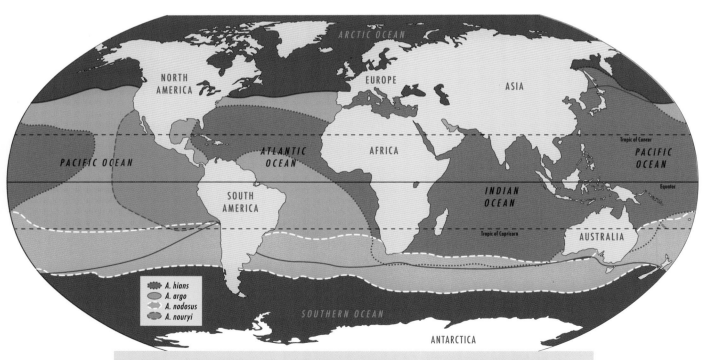

The four currently acknowledged species of argonauts cover the entire globe with their distributions.

predators, the way a decorator crab will plop a stinging anemone on its back as a shield. Argonauts may also be using jellyfish as a portable snack, taking a nibble from time to time. No one has yet figured it out. The relationship would undoubtedly fascinate Jeanne, who loved to observe interactions between species: martens and birds, shrimps and salps, octopuses and pen shells.

Yet another argonaut mystery: Why do they sometimes wash up on beaches in mass strandings of thousands of individuals? This happens from time to time for many species of marine animals; argonauts aren't the only ones. Some marine mammal strandings are caused by disease, and some jellyfish strandings are caused by wind. But when masses of argonauts are found on a beach, no one knows why.

Even the shell of the argonaut itself still holds its puzzles. Although Jeanne proved that argonauts make their own shells, we're still in the dark about exactly how they do it. Scientists have figured out the details of shell production for mollusks that use their mantles to produce shells, such as snails and clams and even nautiluses. But argonauts are the only mollusk, the only animal, in the world that creates a shell with its arms. And we don't know how. A tantalizing clue comes from the blanket octopus, a close relative of argonauts with a similar sex dynamic in which tiny males have detachable hectocotyli and large females have membranous arms. The blanket octopus's membranes are even larger and more dramatic than those of argonauts and can be broken off to distract predators, another case of autonomy. These arms can also apparently secrete a tough material, an ability the female uses right before laying eggs to produce a small rod for egg attachment. Evidence suggests that the rod might even be calcified, like the argonaut's shell.

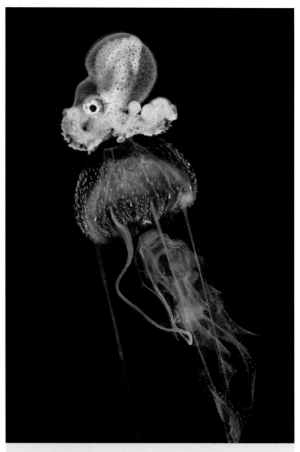

Argonauts seem to make a habit of hitching rides on things, from plant debris to one another's shells and, of course, jellyfish.

Understanding calcification may seem like an esoteric study topic, but in fact it is more urgent than ever, as changing ocean acidity affects the shell-growing ability of animals from plankton to coral. Throughout most of their long evolutionary history, they've had access to calcium carbonate as an abundant resource. Today, oceans absorb huge quantities of the carbon dioxide that humans are pumping into the atmosphere, and this dissolved gas reacts with chemicals in seawater, reducing their availability and making it harder to build shells. So far, cephalopods as a whole seem adaptable enough to survive and thrive in changing oceans, despite rising temperature and acidity. But in this case as in many others, argonauts may be an exception.

The more we learn about the ocean, this enormous environment that envelops nearly two-thirds of our planet, the more we find out how much we have yet to learn. Marine enthusiasts often comment that planet Earth could better be called planet Ocean. We know that the seas affect all human life, providing food even to landlocked cities, oxygen to the entire globe, and climate mitigation without which the planet might be entirely unlivable. But we don't know how many species live in the ocean, how global currents can change, and how intricate ecosystems from coral reefs to deep-sea vents are built.

Although human behavior is fast affecting an ocean we still know so little about, we are also steadily adding to our knowledge, sometimes in a trickle and sometimes in a flood. Explorers and scientists reach literal new depths every year; the deepest octopus ever seen was recorded at 7 kilometers (4.3 miles) in 2020.

If Jeanne could come back today and see what has been discovered since her time, she'd be thrilled to observe all the cephalopod hectocotyli that have been described. She'd probably marvel at the Villepreux-Power Patera, and she'd want to hear all about the chemical signatures of possible life on Venus. And she'd ask us impatiently why we *still* don't know enough about argonauts to raise them in an aquarium.

HOW TO BE A NATURALIST
(OCEAN OBSESSION OPTIONAL)

Has some part of Jeanne's story inspired you? Maybe you'd like to tramp around Sicily collecting caterpillars or study ocean animals in their natural habitat. Those particular activities may be out of reach for now (or they may not!), but no matter where you live it's possible to pursue natural history and connect to the ocean.

Jeanne didn't move to Sicily to become a naturalist. But once she was there, she threw herself into her environment. Any home, no matter how urban or rural, can be explored with the adventurous eyes of a natural historian. You could peer into the corners of an apartment building to catalog insects and spiders or count the squirrels and crows on a power line over the course of a week or a year. You could write a guide like Jeanne's for your backyard.

And if you're lucky enough to live near the sea, well, you may have tide pools and sandy beaches to document and analyze. But even if you're landlocked, as Jeanne of Juillac was when she was growing up, there are ways to get involved with marine biology.

Public aquariums, zoos, and museums offer opportunities to connect with the ocean. They may have volunteer openings or research programs you can participate in. If you find yourself hopelessly enamored of aquatic life, it's even possible to keep a freshwater or saltwater aquarium in your own home—or in a classroom or community center.

Many ocean organizations have online resources to learn more about the ocean and help take care of it. You can organize plastic cleanup days to keep trash out of the water or invent an ocean game to play at school. And one day—who knows?— someone may be writing your biography, describing the unique journey you've traveled. Though there may be tragedy as dire as a shipwreck, may there always be triumph too.

Jeanne's interest in argonauts may well have started with finding a shell like this one on a beach. A simple walk outside can open a world of discovery.

AUTHOR'S NOTE

I fell in love with octopuses on a family trip to the aquarium when I was ten years old. I went home determined to keep my own pet octopus, and with my father's help I installed a secondhand aquarium in my bedroom. My bookshelves became crusted with salt, and the hum of the pumps became my lullaby. Best of all, a little octopus named Serendipity became my friend. She redecorated the aquarium to her taste, learned to recognize which family members participated in feeding, and played tug-of-war with cubes of frozen brine shrimp. I was heartbroken when she died within a year.

Octopuses have short lives, and I was less resilient to their loss than Jeanne. I stopped keeping them as pets, but my love for octopuses grew and deepened until I found myself enamored of all cephalopods, earning a PhD in squid biology, and writing whole books about these amazing animals. I first learned about Jeanne because of her work on argonauts, some of the coolest octopuses around, but when I found out that she'd invented aquariums as well, I felt doubly indebted to her. Jeanne's innovation laid the groundwork for my own transformative experience, staring into an aquarium and watching an octopus watch me back.

The more I learned about Jeanne's life story and the tumultuous period of history that she lived through, the more eager I became to write her biography. Piecing together her life, though, has been a puzzle. Some historical figures leave behind reams of letters and diaries. Not only did Jeanne lose most of her papers in a shipwreck, but it seems she was never inclined to write about her personal life, unless it involved animals. Her affectionate tales of Mignonne the tortoise and the two martens have no counterpart in stories of her siblings, stepmother, or husband.

However, I've been very lucky to be able to build on the work of numerous historians and researchers who've already dug into archives, scanned documents, and laid out timelines. I'm especially grateful to the historian Josquin Debaz for patiently answering my questions, offering his own insights, and reading multiple drafts of the manuscript. Anne-Lan of the Jeanne Villepreux-Power Association has worked tirelessly to compile information about Jeanne and share it with a broader audience, which made my work on this book far easier. Historian Michela D'Angelo also graciously shared her extensive research and helped with many of my questions. If I've still managed to make mistakes, that's on me, not them. And, of course, Claude Arnal kick-started the twenty-first-century revival of Jeanne's story. I only wish that he were still with us to see this biography.

Brief biographies of Jeanne have been published since shortly after her death, but as Debaz pointed out, no one's entirely sure whether these early biographies are reliable.

They don't tell us where their information came from. Did the authors speak to people in Juillac who remembered Jeanne? Did they draw material from her own writing or from the writings of her friends and colleagues? I've tried to do a little better in that regard, using quotes from sources that you can look up yourself, and making it clear wherever I apply a bit of imagination to re-create scenes from Jeanne's life.

My linguistic abilities are not quite on par with hers; I speak only a little French and less Italian. But I'm very fortunate to have friends and colleagues to help in this regard. Cecile Damiron and Arielle Goni O'Kane guided my French, while Manuela Rinaldi and Andrew Packard lent a hand with the Italian. I got some great science help too! Rebecca Helm brought me up to speed on weird argonaut and jelly behaviors, and Brian Engh responded to my befuddlement over how a tortoise could survive three days immersed in alcohol. "I'm not even surprised," he said. "Turtles are gnarly."

The Lady and the Octopus owes its existence to my marvelous agent, Stacey Kondla, who helped me shape the idea for the book and brought it to an incredible editor: Carol Hinz. I'm immensely grateful to Carol, and to the rest of the team at Lerner, for their kind and constructive help. My critique partner Evelyn Strauss and early reader Yael Kisel both provided invaluable encouragement and feedback. Speaking of encouragement, the unflagging support of my spouse, children, and extended family is as crucial to my writing as calcium carbonate is to the construction of an argonaut's shell.

I was drawn to Jeanne because of our shared love for octopuses, but as I learned more about her life, I also became fascinated by our differences. Many scientists find their passion at an early age. However, Jeanne didn't even grow up near the sea, and we have no reason to believe that she conducted experiments or collected wildlife as a child. Some people may fall in love with octopuses at age ten and will still be writing about them at age forty, but others may explore many different interests and professions over the years. Both approaches can lead to a rich and beautiful life.

When I began the research for this book, I hoped I might be able to travel from my California home to the many wonderful places Jeanne lived and worked over her seventy-six years. The COVID-19 pandemic ended that aspiration, but I still dream of roaming the French countryside where she might have watched sheep, dipping my hands into the Mediterranean where she placed her cages, and even catching sight of live argonauts descended from those she studied. Perhaps one day I will. In the meantime, I am deeply grateful to Jeanne for introducing me to her world through her vivid writing, and my new aspiration is that readers find the work of Jeanne Villepreux-Power as illuminating as I did.

TIMELINE

1793   On January 21, in the midst of the French Revolution, King Louis XVI is executed by guillotine.

In September the Reign of Terror begins, as a group of revolutionary politicians led by Maximilien Robespierre begin abusing their power to arrest and execute people on any pretext.

On October 1 Jeanne Nicot and Pierre Villepreux are married in the small town of Juillac, France.

On October 16 Marie Antoinette is guillotined.

1794   On July 28 Robespierre is executed and the Reign of Terror ends, though it is followed by the White Terror, a violent reaction by those who suffered under Robespierre.

Slavery is abolished in all French colonies, but Dominica, home of the three-year-old James Power, was recently transferred from French to British control and will keep an enslaved population until 1833.

On September 25 Jeanne is born in Juillac. She is the first child of Jeanne and Pierre Villepreux. Because she shares her mother's name, she is given the nickname Lili.

1795   On April 7 the formal definition of the metric system is created in France.

Jeanne's father, Pierre, becomes Juillac's first garde champêtre, a position somewhat similar to a police officer.

1796   Georges Cuvier, a member of the French Academy of Sciences, makes the case for extinction, pointing out that the bones of mammoths and mastodons are distinct from those of elephants and must belong to animals that no longer live on Earth.

1799   The French Revolution ends when the army general Napoleon Bonaparte overthrows the revolutionary government and installs himself as first consul (essentially a dictator).

1800   Steam engines are used to industrialize glass polishing, making this material readily available for Jeanne's later aquariums.

1803   On April 26 a meteorite shower in L'Aigle, France, leads the scientist Jean-Baptiste Biot to conclude that the rocks had an extraterrestrial origin.

In May, Britain declares war on France, which many historians consider the start of the Napoleonic Wars. Over the next twelve years, Napoleon wages war with Britain, Austria, Russia, Prussia, Sweden, Portugal, and Spain.

1804   On September 29, four days after Jeanne's tenth birthday, her five-year-old sister Gabrielle dies. Their father mistakenly gives the name of the dead child as Jeanne.

In November, Napoleon is elected emperor of the French.

1805 On August 26 Jeanne's mother dies.

1807 On May 6 Jeanne's father remarries.

1808 Cuvier successfully identifies a fossil mosasaur as a giant marine reptile, followed the next year by his identification of a pterodactyl, a flying reptile. He begins to make the case for an ancient Age of Reptiles.

1811 In England twelve-year-old Mary Anning digs up the first complete skeleton of an ichthyosaur, another giant marine reptile.

1812 At the age of seventeen, Jeanne walks from Juillac to Paris. Her trip is broken by a stop in Orléans. When she arrives in Paris, she becomes a milliner's assistant.

1815 Napoleon's army is defeated by the British and their allies at the Battle of Waterloo. Napoleon gives up his position as emperor, and King Louis XVIII returns to the throne of France.

1816 On June 17 King Louis's nephew marries a Sicilian princess, Maria Carolina di Borbone. Jeanne sews the princess's wedding gown and meets the Irish merchant James Power, now working from Sicily.

1818 On March 4 Jeanne and James are married in Messina, Sicily.

1819 Georges Cuvier is given the title of baron in honor of his scientific work.

1820 Sicilians revolt against King Ferdinand I, who rules the joint kingdoms of Sicily and Naples. The Austrian army helps him suppress the insurrection.

1821 English inventor Michael Faraday demonstrates the first electric motor. With no electrical grid to plug into and impractically expensive batteries, electric motors won't come into regular use until the end of the century.

1822 Henri de Blainville coins the term *paleontology*.

1824 The Gioenia Academy of Catania, a scientific society, is founded in Catania, Sicily, a city 88 kilometers (55 miles) south of Messina.

1829 Cuvier names the "parasitic worm" inside a female argonaut's shell *Hectocotylus octopodis*.

1830 Mary Anning is struggling financially. Her friend and fellow geologist paints the first "aquarium view" paleoart, *Duria Antiquior, a More Ancient Dorset*, and sells prints to raise money for Anning.

A second French revolution, sometimes called the July Revolution, ousts one king and installs another.

1832 Jeanne invents her first aquariums and begins using them to study marine animals in her home.

The first diver to successfully carry compressed air to breathe underwater, rather than breathing from a tube connected to a surface supply, dies in New York City's East River when his diving tube breaks.

1833   In September, Jeanne experiments on shell repair in argonauts. Most of the animals die after she breaks their shells, but those who survive demonstrate a skillful capacity for mending.

The first electric telegraph is used over a distance of 1 kilometer (0.6 miles) in Germany.

1834   Jeanne presents the results of her argonaut studies to the Gioenia Academy.

1835   Commander Alban de Gasquet visits Jeanne and James in Messina and suggests that Jeanne send her work to a colleague in Paris, who could present it to the Academy of Sciences. Jeanne agrees, and her work is passed along to Sander Rang.

Jeanne is elected the first female member of the Gioenia Academy, and her inventions are named Power cages.

1836   Jeanne's argonaut research is published in the journal of the Academy of Catania, with support from Carmelo Maravigna.

1837   On January 7 Alessio Scigliani praises Jeanne's work in the *Hobby Journal for Ladies*.

Rang presents Jeanne's work as his own to the French Academy of Sciences, and Blainville publishes a counterargument.

The Zoological Society of London officially names Jeanne's invention the Power cage.

Jeanne and James travel to London, making arrangements for Jeanne's collections to be sent after them by ship.

1838   The ship containing Jeanne's collections sinks.

James has been ill, and doctors in London advise his return to Sicily. The couple visits Messina again.

Anastasio Cocco names a deep-sea fish after Jeanne, *Gonostomus poweriae* (now *Vinciguerria poweriae*).

1839   Back in London, Jeanne hosts visits from Richard and Caroline Owen, and Richard presents her argonaut research at the London Zoological Society. Jeanne is admitted as a corresponding member of the society and invited to publish in its *Magazine of Natural History*.

Her first book about Sicily, *Itinerario della Sicilia*, is published in Messina. Jeanne returns at the end of the year and conducts more argonaut experiments, as well as completing her watercolor painting of an argonaut.

The early photograph technique of daguerreotypes becomes available to the public.

1840   Blainville publicly admits his error and acknowledges Jeanne's proof that the argonaut is the builder of its own shell.

On September 7 Jeanne's father, Pierre Villepreux, dies.

1841 On January 29, in Messina, Jeanne makes an official will, leaving everything to James. She is forty-six years old.

1842 Jeanne's *Guida per la Sicilia*, an expanded and corrected version of her *Itinerario*, is published.

James and Jeanne move to Paris. They will continue to travel between France, England, and Italy.

Richard Owen coins the word *dinosaur*.

Albert von Kölliker travels to Messina and picks up Jeanne's work on the hectocotylus.

1844 Jeanne visits Naples, Italy, and gives her family inheritance to her brother Joseph.

1845 While in London, Jeanne purchases land for her brother in Juillac.

Kölliker publishes his hectocotylus research, supporting Jeanne's idea that the "worms" are male argonauts.

1848 Another French Revolution, the February Revolution, removes the monarch that had been installed in 1830. A new republic begins, and Napoleon's nephew, Napoleon III, is elected president.

1849 Anna Thynne keeps corals in her home, in the world's first marine aquarium with a balance of plants and animals.

1851 A submarine telegraph cable is laid between England and France, with the first successful communication between the two countries in October.

In November or December, two waterspouts move from the sea across the island of Sicily, becoming one of the deadliest tornadoes in recorded history.

A species list is published including *Carcinococcus poweriae*, the barrel shrimp named after Jeanne that will later be recognized as *Phronima sedentaria*.

1852 The hectocotylus is correctly described as a detachable arm of the male argonaut.

Napoleon III leverages his position as president into being "elected" emperor.

James becomes secretary of the Society of the Submarine Telegraph between France and England.

1853 The first public aquarium, the Fish House at the London Zoo, is created by Philip Henry Gosse, who shortens "aquatic vivarium" to "aquarium."

1856 Jeanne publishes her most complete paper on argonaut research, including all her experiments from her time in Sicily.

1857 As "aquariophily" spreads throughout Europe, Jeanne writes to Richard Owen about her "rights as inventor" of the aquarium.

1858 Richard Owen credits Jeanne's work with aquariums in his article about mollusks for the *Encyclopaedia Britannica*.

1859   On November 24, Charles Darwin's *On the Origin of Species* is published.

A marine station is established for aquaculture in Concarneau, France, the oldest marine laboratory that's still active today.

1860   Jeanne publishes her diverse studies on animal behavior, including her martens and tortoise as well as barrel shrimp, snails, and sea stars.

1861   Jeanne and James have their photographic portraits taken by Disdéri.

1867   Jeanne publishes her final paper, on meteorology.

1870   On July 16 France declares war on Prussia. The Prussian army mobilizes quickly and invades France on August 4.

As the Prussian army approaches Paris, Jeanne leaves the city for her hometown of Juillac. James stays behind, in his telegraph post.

On September 19 the Prussian army closes around Paris, preventing food or any other supplies from going into the city.

1871   On January 25 Jeanne dies in Juillac. She is seventy-six years old.

On January 28, France surrenders. The Prussian army immediately sends food into Paris and withdraws its army.

On May 15 James buys a plot in the Juillac cemetery.

1872   On January 9, less than a year after losing Jeanne, James dies at the age of eighty. He is buried with his wife in Juillac.

1875   The Treaty of the Meter, or Convention du Metre, is signed in Paris by seventeen countries, including the United States. It creates the International Bureau of Weights and Measures to standardize measurements and ensure that metric units like meter and kilogram have the same meaning in every country.

1888   Alphonse Rebière writes the first, brief biography of Jeanne.

1997   A crater on Venus is named the Villepreux-Power Patera to honor Jeanne.

GLOSSARY

ammonites: extinct cephalopods that grew external shells, often coiled

anatomy: the structure of a body and its parts

aquarium: a water-filled container built to maintain aquatic life

aragonite: the crystal form of calcium carbonate that most mollusks use to make their shells, along with calcite

biologist: a scientist who studies any form of life, from plants and animals to fungi and bacteria

brood: to care for eggs until hatching

calcium carbonate: the main building block of mollusk shells, which the animals create by gathering raw ingredients dissolved in the surrounding seawater

cephalopod: the group of mollusks that contains octopuses, squids, cuttlefish, and nautiluses, as well as many extinct species

chemise à la reine: a style of dress popularized by Marie Antoinette, queen of France, which was lighter and more casual than her typical fashion

convent: a community of nuns living together

crustaceans: the group of animals that contains crabs, lobsters, and shrimp

daguerreotype: a very early type of photograph produced on a sheet of copper

evolution: the process of life changing and diversifying over generations due to natural selection

experimentalism: the practice of seeking knowledge through tests and demonstrations

extinction: the death of all members of a group of organisms, most often a species

Fata Morgana: an optical illusion that makes land or cities seem to appear over water

filter feeder: a marine animal that uses part of its body to filter small particles from the water and then eat them

fixative: a chemical solution that can preserve a dead organism indefinitely

hectocotylus: the modified arm of a male cephalopod, used to transfer sperm

hypothesis: an idea that can be tested

imperial system: a term commonly used to describe any system of measurement than uses feet, pounds, and degrees Fahrenheit, although there are slight differences between true imperial units and US customary units

lingua franca: the language used to communicate by members of a group with different native languages

malacological: related to malacology, the study of mollusks

mantle: the main part of a cephalopod's body, which contains all the animal's organs

metric system: the system of measurement most commonly used in Europe, which includes meters, kilograms, and degrees Celsius

mollusk: a group of soft-bodied animals, many of which grow shells, which includes snails, slugs, clams, and cephalopods

naturalist: a person who studies animals, plants, rocks, and the natural world; what Jeanne and her colleagues called themselves; also known as a natural historian

paleontologist: a scientist who studies fossils, a term coined by Henri de Blainville

patera: the craterlike vent on top of a volcano

polymath: a person with knowledge or expertise in a wide range of fields

regeneration: an organism's ability to regrow part of its body that has been damaged or removed

scientist: a person who studies one or more of the branches of science, such as biology, chemistry, or physics; a term coined in 1834 and not widely used until many years later

siphon: the part of a cephalopod's body used to squirt water; also called a funnel

spawn: to lay eggs

waterspouts: tornadoes formed over water that can sometimes move onto land

zoologist: a biologist who focuses on animals

SOURCE NOTES

10 "The mollusk when . . . forming its shell": Jeannette Power, "Observations on the Poulp of the Argonaut," *Magazine of Natural History*, March 1839, 151, https://www.google.com/books/edition/The_Magazine_of_Natural_History/Q_YWAAAAYAAJ?hl=en&gbpv=0.

13 "The American economy . . . meters a 'mile'": Russ Rowlett, "English Customary Weights and Measures," ibiblio.org, April 26, 2018, http://www.ibiblio.org/units/custom.html.

17 "a letter that . . . servant lili villepreux": Jeanne Villepreux-Power, to the mayor of Juillac, April 5, 1812, translated by the author with help from Josquin Debaz. Scans received via e-mail March 2, 2020.

23 "I have found . . . with experimental observations": Jeanne Villepreux-Power, *Observations physiques sur le poulpe de l'Argonauta argo: commencées en 1832 et terminées en 1843, dédiées à M. le professeur Owen F.R.S.* (Paris: Charles de Mourgues Frères, 1856), 3, https://archive.org/details/b2228476x/.

24 "scenes of open . . . in the world": Jeanne Villepreux-Power, *Guida per la Sicilia* (Naples: Dallo Stabilimento Poligrafico di Filippo Cirelli, 1842), 1–2.

24–25 "A sumptuous maritime . . . remains partly unfinished": Villepreux-Power, 2.

26 "took [Jeanne] to . . . marry her later": Alphonse Rebière, "Madame Power: Une Naturaliste Oubliée," *Bulletin de la société des lettres de la Corrèze*, 1899, 305.

27 "Mrs. Power, despite . . . be a genius": Alessio Scigliani, "Madama Jeannette Power," *Passatempo per le Dame* I, 1837, http://jeanne-villepreux-power.org/sa-notoriete/articles-qui-parlent-d-elle-de-son-vivant/86-article-du-professeur-scigliani-sur-jeannette-power.

28 "Rarely, we can . . . who work there": Villepreux-Power, *Guida per la Sicilia*, 1.

29 "I have traveled . . . and antiquity collections": Jeannette Power, *Observations sur l'origine des corps météoriques, aérolithes, bolides ou pierres qu'on dit tombées du ciel* (Paris: A. Chaix, 1867), 8.

30 "there is no lesser . . . and rare plants": Villepreux-Power, *Guida per la Sicilia*, 33.

30 "worthy of the . . . of the artists": Villepreux-Power, 34.

30 "composed of a . . . of fossil shells": Villepreux-Power, 34.

30 "minerals, fossils, agates, . . . from its chrysalis": Jeanne Villepreux-Power, *Observations et expériences physiques sur la Bulla lignaria, l'Astérias, l'Octopus vulgaris et la Pinna nobilis, la reproduction des testacés univalves marins, moeurs du Crustacé powerii, moeurs de la martre commune, faits curieux d'une tortue, l'Argonauta argo, plan d'étude pour les animaux marins, faits curieux d'une chenille* (Paris: Charles de Mourgues Frères, 1860), 7.

31 "For several years . . . died in its ear": Villepreux-Power, 7–8.

31–32 "Its stem is . . . or around Paris": Villepreux-Power, 7–8.

35 "I had composed . . . with this liquor": Villepreux-Power, 27.

36 "I had a tortoise . . . like a lot": Villepreux-Power, 27.

36 "After a few . . . gave her dessert": Villepreux-Power, 27.

37 "They took me . . . always near me": Villepreux-Power, 18.

37–38 "Shortly after the . . . disgust and repugnance": Villepreux-Power, 18–19.

38 "I got myself . . . pieces and devoured": Villepreux-Power, 19–20.

38 "I promised them . . . brought me eleven": Villepreux-Power, 22.

38 "on seeing the birds . . . they could catch": Villepreux-Power, 22.

38 "At first they . . . a thousand antics": Villepreux-Power, 19.

38 "If a dog . . . approach my house": Villepreux-Power, 21–22.

38 "they never tried . . . them a beating": Villepreux-Power, 26.

40 "As they passed . . . was soon done": Villepreux-Power, 24.

40 "As I was going . . . peace was made": Villepreux-Power, 25.

41 "As I was . . . as an inventor": Jeanne Villepreux-Power, to Richard Owen, August 21, 1857.

41 "To Madam Jeannette . . . of molluscous animals": Richard Owen, "Mollusca," *Encyclopaedia Britannica*, 8th ed., 328, https://digital.nls.uk/encyclopaedia -britannica/archive/193596964#?c =0&m=0&s=0&cv=341&xywh =2211%2C474%2C3726%2C2765.

41 "Here, having crossed . . . invented by poets": Villepreux-Power, *Guida per la Sicilia*, 1.

43 "illustrious naturalist, whom . . . replace them backwards": Villepreux-Power, *Observations physiques sur le poulpe de l'Argonauta argo*, 8.

43 "This is the . . . by the second": Villepreux-Power, 271.

43 "The fisherman have . . . accommodating to me": Villepreux-Power, *Observations et expériences*, 3.

44 "a little money . . . them than money": Villepreux-Power, *Guida per la Sicilia*, 270.

44 "From 1832 to . . . name of 'cages'": Jeannette Power, "XXXI.—Observations on the Habits of Various Marine Animals," *Annals and Magazine of Natural History* 20, no. 119 (1857): 334.

45 "unique architectural features . . . at both ends": Peter Forsskål, *Descriptiones Animalium, Avium, Amphibiorum, Piscium, Insectorum, Vermium; quae in Itinere Orientali Observavit Petrus Forskål. Post Mortem Auctoris editit Carsten Niebuhr. Adjuncta est materia Medica Kahirina* (Hafniae: Mölleri, 1775), 95–96.

47 "The first two . . . the previous ones": P. A. Latreille, *Histoire naturelle, générale et particulière, des Crustacés et des Insectes*, vol. 6 (Paris: Dufart An X, 1803), 291, in Carl Bovallius, *Contributions to a Monograph of the Amphipoda Hyperiidea*, vol. 1–2 (Stockholm: Norstedt 1887), 362.

47–48 "The crustacean deposits . . . after their birth": Villepreux-Power, *Observations et expériences*, 15–16.

48 "I could not . . . incomplete": Villepreux-Power, 16.

50 "facilitated by the . . . a nutritive pulp": Power, "XXXI.—Observations on the Habits of Various Marine Animals," 335.

50 "increasing the size . . . with the biggest": Villepreux-Power, *Observations et expériences*, 10–11.

52 "These I deposited . . . lazzaretto of Messina": Villepreux-Power, *Observations physiques sur le poulpe de l'Argonauta argo*, 6.

52 "Regeneration studies can . . . all experimental biology": T. S. Okada, "A Brief History of Regeneration Research— For Admiring Professor Niazi's Discovery of the Effect of Vitamin A on Regeneration," *Journal of Biosciences* 21, no. 3 (1996): 263.

53 "expressed confidence that . . . for the worse": Okada, 264.

53 "I removed the . . . gave me shivers": Villepreux-Power, *Observations et expériences*, 13–14.

54 "Eight days later . . . to any result": Villepreux-Power, 14.

54 "Great was my . . . 12 millimeters long": Villepreux-Power , 14.

55 "having devoured the . . . of the cage": Villepreux-Power, *Observations physiques sur le poulpe de l'Argonauta argo*, 21.

57 "One day when . . . devour the mollusc": Villepreux-Power, *Observations et expériences*, 11.

57 "It would require . . . and eats it": Villepreux-Power, 12.

58 "I never thought . . . with happy success": Villepreux-Power, *Observations physiques sur le poulpe de l'Argonauta argo*, 7.

59 "Extending backwards its . . . as a rudder": Pliny the Elder, "The Nautilus, or Sailing Polypus," *The Natural History*, London. Taylor and Francis, 1855, http://www .perseus.tufts.edu/hopper/text?doc =Perseus%3Atext%3A1999.02.0137% 3Abook%3D9%3Achapter%3D47.

63 "I perceived that . . . this interesting point": Villepreux-Power, *Observations physiques sur le poulpe de l'Argonauta argo*, 6.

63 "a net bag . . . on each side": Villepreux-Power, 7. "Angamo" is misspelled as "ungamo."

64 "We must be . . . water remain constant": Villepreux-Power, 19.

64 "another ploy . . . of the siphon": Villepreux-Power, 11.

65 "The sea is . . . right and left": Villepreux-Power, 10.

66 "Now I imagine . . . it finds it": Benjamin Franklin, William Brownrigg, and Farish, "Of the Stilling of Waves by Means of Oil. Extracted from Sundry Letters between Benjamin Franklin, LL. D. F. R. S., William Brownrigg, M. D. F. R. S., and the Reverend Mr. Farish," *Philosophical Transactions* 64 (1774): 453.

67 "When the air . . . of an eye": Villepreux-Power, *Observations physiques sur le poulpe de l'Argonauta argo*, 12.

67 "almost as flexible as the first": Villepreux-Power, 13.

68 "The little octopus . . . of the shell": Villepreux-Power, 14.

68 "The human understanding . . . agree with it": Francis Bacon, *Novum Organum*, 1620, in E. A. Burtt, ed., *The English Philosophers from Bacon to Mill* (New York: Random House, 1939), 36, in Raymond Nickerson, "Confirmation Bias: A Ubiquitous Phenomenon in Many Guises," *Review of General Psychology* 2, no. 2 (1998): 176.

69 "not wanting to . . . begun its shell": Villepreux-Power, *Observations physiques sur le poulpe de l'Argonauta argo*, 15.

70 "One must see . . . at the beginning,": Villepreux-Power, 15.

70–71 "I have no . . . a gelatinous substance": Villepreux-Power, 16.

71 "These poor animals . . . without their shells": Villepreux-Power, 21.

72 "If [the argonaut] . . . arms, it survived": Villepreux-Power, 9.

72 "though not the poor birds": Villepreux-Power, *Observations et expériences*, 22–23.

72 "as a result . . . series of wounds": Ivan Pavlov, quoted in Michael Specter, "Drool: Ivan Pavlov's Real Quest," *New Yorker*, November 17, 2014, https://www.newyorker.com/magazine/2014/11/24/drool.

74 "When the rays . . . are really beautiful": Villepreux-Power, *Observations physiques sur le poulpe de l'Argonauta argo*, 12.

75 "It was useless . . . make these experiments": Villepreux-Power, 22.

78 "Giovanna Power [is] . . . great Giovanna Power": Francesco Aldaresi, "Guide de la Sicile, Ouvrage de Giovanna Power, née Villepreux, Naples, Cirelli, 1842," Jeanne Villepreux-Power Association, February 16, 2014, http://jeanne-villepreux-power.org/sa-notoriete/articles-qui-parlent-d-elle-de-son-vivant/87-article-de-francesco-aldaresi-sur-le-guide-de-la-sicile.

79 "founded on a . . . observation of nature": "The American Cyclopædia (1879)/Müller, Johannes," Wikisource, accessed January 13, 2022, https://en.wikisource.org/wiki/The_American_Cyclop%C3%A6dia_(1879)/M%C3%BCller,_Johannes.

80 " 'Asiaticus' . . . 'sluggish' ": Isabelle Charmantier, "Linnaeus and Race," Linnean Society of London, September 3, 2020, https://www.linnean.org/learning/who-was-linnaeus/linnaeus-and-race.

80 "Scientific writers, not . . . what is popular": Frederick Douglass, "The Claims of the Negro Ethnologically Considered: An Address Delivered in Hudson, Ohio, 12 July 1854," *The Speeches of Frederick Douglass: A Critical Edition*, eds. John R. McKivigan and Julie Husband (New Haven, CT: Yale University Press, 2018), 133.

81 "prudens magis quam loquax": Mario Alberghina, "The Unsolved Mystery of the Current Seal of Gioeni's Academy," *Bulletin of the Gioenia Academy of Natural Sciences of Catania* 49, no. 379 (2016): FP81–FP90, http://bollettino.gioenia.it/index.php/gioenia/article/view/22.

83 "Having received . . . a stubborn silence": Villepreux-Power, *Observations physiques sur le poulpe de l'Argonauta argo*, 27.

84–85 "that the animal . . . belong to it": André Marie Constant Duméril and Henri de Blainville, "Report of a Notice, by M. Rang, Respecting the Inhabitant of the Argonaut," *The Magazine of Natural History and Journal of Zoology, Botany, Mineralogy, Geology and Meteorology* (London: Longman, Orme, Brown, Green, and Longmans, 1837), 393.

86 "among the richest . . . singular of Europe":
Michela Di Angelo, "Da 'Cenerentola'
a 'Dama degli Argonauti': Jeannette
Villepreux Power a Messina (1818–1843),"
Naturalista Sicil S 4 (2012): 36, 201.

87 "January 12th. We . . . was practically
settled": Caroline Owen, diary extracts in
Richard Owen, *The Life of Richard Owen*,
vol. 1 (New York: D. Appleton, 1894),
152–153.

87 "26th. R and I . . . match the rest": Owen,
153.

88 "February 2. —R. to Madame . . . discover
these things": Owen, 153–154.

88 "Just as I . . . herring and toast": Owen,
240–241.

90 "The cause of . . . again for England":
Jeannette Power to Professor Antonio De
Giacomo, February 22, 1838, in Di Angelo,
"Da 'Cenerentola,'" 36, 201.

91 "In the confusion . . . these studies
resurface": Power, "Observations on
the Habits of Various Marine Animals,"
334–335.

93 "Waterspouts would have . . . to the
ground": Power, *Observations sur l'origine*, 7.

94 "I am amazed . . . in the future": Carmelo
Maravigna, "Ragguaglio delle Osservazioni
ed esperienze fatte sullo Argonauta Argo
L. da Mad. Jeannette Power," *Giornale di
Scienze, Lettere ed Arti*, May 1836, 6.

97 "as everyone knows . . . as a sail": Power,
"Observations on the Poulp," 103.

99 "I have read . . . my inventor rights":
Jeanne Villepreux-Power, to Richard
Owen, August 21, 1857.

99–100 "the Hypothesis that . . . an anal orifice":
Albert Kölliker, "II. Some Observations
upon the Structure of Two New Species
of Hectocotyle, Parasitic upon *Tremoctopus
violaceus*, D. Ch., and Argonauta Argo,
Linn.; with an Exposition of the Hypothesis
That These Hectocotylæ Are the Males of
the Cephalopoda upon Which They Are
Found," *Transactions of the Linnean Society of
London* 1 (1846): 9.

100 "drop off on . . . *Hectocotylus Octopodis* of
Cuvier": Heinrich Müller, "Upon the
Male of *Argonauta Argo* and the *Hectocotyli*,"
Arthur Henfrey and Thomas Henry Huxley,
eds., in *Scientific Memoirs: Selected from the
Transactions of Foreign Academies of Science,
and from Foreign Journals. Natural History*
(London: Taylor & Francis, 1853), 53.

100 "very desirous of . . . of independent
animality": Müller, 53–56.

100 "Sailing Cuttle Fish": *The National
Encyclopædia. A Dictionary of Universal
Knowledge. By Writers of Eminence in
Literature, Science, and Art*, ed. J. H. F.
Brabner (London: William Mackenzie,
1884–1888).

102 "The rivers of . . . as the lakes": Villepreux-
Power, *Observations et expériences*, 4.

102 "When the small . . . transport them
elsewhere": Villepreux-Power, 5.

106 "you know what . . . for my departure":
Villepreux-Power, to the mayor of Juillac.

107 "Each twenty years . . . a woman scientist":
Josquin Debaz, in a discussion with the
author, August 18, 2020.

107 "Many features on . . . of the honor":
Magellan Press Releases, "Public Invited to
Name Features on Venus," Jet Propulsion
Laboratory, March 8, 1991, https://www2
.jpl.nasa.gov/magellan/pr1353.html.

107–108 "I thought that . . . *Guida per la Sicilia*":
Michela d'Angela, in an email to the
author, August 31, 2021.

108 "He will be . . . for them both": Anne-Lan,
"Annonce du décés de Claude Arnal," July
2020, email to the author, September 9, 2020.

109 "The spectrum of . . . of the aquarium":
Debaz, discussion with the author.

109 "I think the . . . for her time": Debaz.

109 "She had to . . . cannot be trusted": Debaz.

110 "My unexpected departure . . . be
extremely so": Villepreux-Power,
Observations et expériences, 6–7.

117 "I'm not even . . . Turtles are gnarly": Brian
Engh, in a conversation with the author on
Twitter, August 13, 2020.

BIBLIOGRAPHY

Chapter 1

Arnal, Claude. "La Dame des Argonautes." *Bulletin de la Société des Lettres, Sciences et Arts de la Corrèze*, 1994, 179–189.

Benham, Elizabeth. "Busting Myths about the Metric System." *Taking Measure* (blog), National Institute of Standards and Technology, October 6, 2020. https://www.nist.gov/blogs/taking -measure/busting-myths-about-metric-system.

Bergin, Hannah. "How France Became the Fashion Capital of the World." Culture Trip, April 12, 2018. https://theculturetrip.com/europe/france/articles/how-france-became-the-fashion-capital -of-the-world/.

De Nussac, Louis. "Pour un tombeau abandonné." *La République*, November 8, 1911.

Lefebure, Nadine. *Femmes océanes: Les grandes pionnières maritimes.* Grenoble, France: Glénat, 1995.

"Marie-Caroline of Bourbon-Two Sicilies, Duchess of Berry," Wikipedia. Last modified November 16, 2019. https://en.wikipedia.org/wiki/Marie-Caroline_of_Bourbon-Two_Sicilies,_Duchess_ of_Berry.

Rebière, Alphonse, "Madame Power: Une Naturaliste Oubliée." *Bulletin de la société des lettres de la Corrèze*, 1899, 303–329.

Rowlett, Russ. "English Customary Weights and Measures." ibiblio.org, April 26, 2018. http://www .ibiblio.org/units/custom.html.

"Sa vie date par date." Jeanne Villepreux-Power Association. Last modified February 14, 2014. http:// jeanne-villepreux-power.org/sa-vie/sa-vie-date-par-date.

"A Stitch in Time S01E06 Marie Antoinette." YouTube video, 28:55. Posted by BBC, February 12, 2018. https://www.youtube.com/watch?v=fN4RQiYPSqM&feature=youtu.be.

Chapter 2

Chatfield, Chris. "Waterspouts." Gallery of Natural Phenomena. Accessed January 13, 2022. http:// www.phenomena.org.uk/tornadoes/page6/page6.html.

Ebrahim, Margaret. "Exotic Pets in U.S. May Pose Health Risk." AP News, November 27, 2006. Accessed January 13, 2022. https://apnews.com/article/4cf51153a228e79b1cdf3a4a9188e8cd.

"Georges Cuvier." Wikipedia. Last modified June 30, 2020. https://en.wikipedia.org/wiki /Georges_Cuvier.

"Maria Sibylla Merian." Wikipedia. Last modified September 2, 2020. https://en.wikipedia.org /wiki/Maria_Sibylla_Merian.

"Mary Anning." Wikipedia. Last modified September 26, 2020. https://en.wikipedia.org/wiki /Mary_Anning.

Mormino, Vincenzo. "Hermann's Tortoise in Sicily," Best of Sicily Magazine. Accessed January 13, 2022. http://www.bestofsicily.com/mag/art46.htm.

Power, Jeannette. *Observations et expériences physiques sur plusieurs animaux marins et terrestres*. Paris: Charles de Mourgues Frères, 1860.

Schapiro, Rich. "Bad Timing! 'Keeping Up' Star Kim Kardashian Says She's Sorry for Photos of Suzy, Her Chimp." *New York Daily News*, February 24, 2009.

Scigliani, Alessio. "Madama Jeannette Power." *Passatempo per le Dame* I, 1837. http://jeanne-villepreux-power.org/sa-notoriete/articles-qui-parlent-d-elle-de-son-vivant/86-article-du-professeur-scigliani-sur-jeannette-power.

Villepreux-Power, Jeanne. *Guida per la Sicilia*. Naples: Dallo Stabilimento Poligrafico di Filippo Cirelli, 1842.

———. *Observations et expériences physiques sur la Bulla lignaria, l'Astérias, l'Octopus vulgaris et la Pinna nobilis, la reproduction des testacés univalves marins, moeurs du Crustacé powerii, moeurs de la martre commune, faits curieux d'une tortue, l'Argonauta argo, plan d'étude pour les animaux marins, faits curieux d'une chenille*. Paris: Charles de Mourgues Frères, 1860.

———. *Observations physiques sur le poulpe de l'Argonauta argo: commencées en 1832 et terminées en 1843, dédiées à M. le professeur Owen F.R.S.* Paris: Charles de Mourgues Frères, 1856.

———. *Observations sur l'origine des corps météoriques, aérolithes, bolides ou pierres qu'on dit tombées du ciel*. Paris: A. Chaix, 1867.

Chapter 3

Baker, A. de C. "The Problem of Keeping Planktonic Animals Alive in the Laboratory." *Journal of the Marine Biological Association of the United Kingdom* 43, no. 2 (1963): 291–294.

Bay-Nouailhat, A. "Description of *Scaphander lignarius*." Mer et Littoral, May 2007. http://www.european-marine-life.org/14/scaphander-lignarius.php.

Breure, Abraham S. H. "The Sound of a Snail: Two Cases of Acoustic Defence in Gastropods." *Journal of Molluscan Studies* 81, no. 2 (2015): 290–293.

"Diving History Wayback Page." Diving Heritage. Last modified October 22, 2004. https://www.divingheritage.com/wayback.htm#:~:text=On%20his%20last%20dive%2C%20in,cause%20given%20for%20his%20demise.

Finn, Julian K., Tom Tregenza, and Mark D. Norman. "Defensive Tool Use in a Coconut-Carrying Octopus." *Current Biology* 19, no. 23 (2009): R1069–R1070.

"History of Underwater Diving." Wikipedia. Last modified September 10, 2020. https://en.wikipedia.org/wiki/History_of_underwater_diving.

"Lazzaretto of Messina." History of Medicine Topographical Database. Accessed September 30, 2020. http://himetop.wikidot.com/lazzaretto-of-messina.

Lefebure, Nadine. *Femmes océanes: Les grandes pionnières maritimes*. Grenoble, France: Glénat, 1995.

Mann, Janet, and Eric M. Patterson. "Tool Use by Aquatic Animals." *Philosophical Transactions of the Royal Society B: Biological Sciences* 368, no. 1630 (2013): 20120424.

Newmyer, Stephen T. "Tool Use in Animals: Ancient and Modern Insights and Moral Consequences." *Scholia: Studies in Classical Antiquity* 14, no. 1 (2005): 3–17.

Power, Jeannette. "XXXI.—Observations on the Habits of Various Marine Animals." *Annals and Magazine of Natural History* 20, no. 119 (1857): 334–336.

Richter, Jonas N., Binyamin Hochner, and Michael J. Kuba. "Pull or Push? Octopuses Solve a Puzzle Problem." *PloS One* 11, no. 3 (2016): e0152048.

Seed, Amanda, and Richard Byrne. "Animal Tool-Use." *Current Biology* 20, no. 23 (2010): R1032–R1039.

Taylor, Alex H., and Russell D. Gray. "Animal Cognition: Aesop's Fable Flies from Fiction to Fact." *Current Biology* 19, no. 17 (2009): R731–R732.

Chapter 4

Andrews, Paul L. R. "Laboratory Invertebrates: Only Spineless, or Spineless and Painless." *ILAR Journal* 52, no. 2 (2011): 121–125.

Behroozi, Peter, Kimberly Cordray, William Griffin, and Feredoon Behroozi. "The Calming Effect of Oil on Water." *American Journal of Physics* 75, no. 5 (2007): 407–414.

Crook, Robyn J. "Behavioral and Neurophysiological Evidence Suggests Affective Pain Experience in Octopus." *iScience* 24, no. 3 (2021): 102229.

Mertens, Joost. "Oil on Troubled Waters: Benjamin Franklin and the Honor of Dutch Seamen." *PhT* 59, no. 1 (2006): 36.

NOVA: What the Physics?! "How Oil Calms Waves." PBS. Accessed September 30, 2020. https://www.pbslearningmedia.org/resource/nvwtp-sci-oilwaves/wgbh-nova-what-the-physics-how-oil-calms-waves/support-materials/.

Pliny the Elder. "The Nautilus, or Sailing Polypus." *Natural History.* Accessed January 13, 2022. http://www.perseus.tufts.edu/hopper/text?doc=Perseus%3Atext%3A1999.02.0137%3Abook%3D9%3Achapter%3D47.

Specter, Michael. "Drool: Ivan Pavlov's Real Quest." *New Yorker*, November 17, 2014. https://www.newyorker.com/magazine/2014/11/24/drool.

Staaf, Danna. *Monarchs of the Sea.* New York: Experiment, 2020.

"When Vegetable Oils Spill." *Washington Post*, July 17, 1993.

Chapter 5

Aldaresi, Francesco. "Guide de la Sicile: Ouvrage de Giovanna Power, née Villepreux; Naples—Cirelli—1842. Jeanne Villepreux-Power Association, February 16, 2014. http://jeanne-villepreux-power.org/sa-notoriete/articles-qui-parlent-d-elle-de-son-vivant/87-article-de-francesco-aldaresi-sur-le-guide-de-la-sicile.

Allcock, A. Louise, Sigurd von Boletzky, Laure Bonnaud-Ponticelli, Norma E. Brunetti, Néstor J. Cazzaniga, Eric Hochberg, Marcela Ivanovic et al. "The Role of Female Cephalopod Researchers: Past and Present." *Journal of Natural History* 49, no. 21–24 (2015): 1235–1266.

"The American Cyclopædia (1879)/Müller, Johannes." Wikisource. Accessed January 13, 2022. https://en.wikisource.org/wiki/The_American_Cyclop%C3%A6dia_(1879)/M%C3%BCller,_Johannes.

Groeben C. "Tourists in Science: 19th Century Research Trips to the Mediterranean." *Proc Calif Acad Sci.* 59, suppl. I (2008): 139–154.

Wright, John. *The Naming of the Shrew: A Curious History of Latin Names.* London: Bloomsbury, 2015.

Chapter 6

Arnal, Claude. "Jeanne Villepreux-Power: A Pioneering Experimental Malacologist." *Bulletin of the Malacological Society of London.* Accessed January 13, 2022. http://www.malacsoc.org.uk /malacological_bulletin/BULL34/JEANNE.htm.

Artichoke. *26 Scientists Volume Two: Newton–Zeno.* CD. Self-released by Artichoke, May 14, 2009.

Brian, A. W., and E. R. Stofan. "Geology of the V39 Quadrangle: Taussig, Venus." (2000). Lunar and Planetary Science XXXI. https://www.lpi.usra.edu/meetings/lpsc2000/pdf/1664.pdf.

Clary, Renee M., and James H. Wandersee. "Through the Looking Glass: The History of Aquarium Views and Their Potential to Improve Learning in Science Classrooms." *Science & Education* 14, no. 6 (2005): 579–596.

Duneton, Claude. *La dame de l'Argonaute.* Paris: Denoël, 2009.

"International Historic Chemical Landmarks: Discovery of Oxygen by Joseph Priestley." American Chemical Society. Accessed September 30, 2020. http://www.acs.org/content/acs/en/education /whatischemistry/landmarks/josephpriestleyoxygen.html.

Kölliker, Albert. "II. Some Observations upon the Structure of Two New Species of Hectocotyle, Parasitic upon *Tremoctopus violaceus*, D. Ch., and Argonauta Argo, Linn.; with an Exposition of the Hypothesis That These Hectocotylæ Are the Males of the Cephalopoda upon Which They Are Found." *Transactions of the Linnean Society of London* 1 (1846): 9–21.

Magellan Press Releases. "Public Invited to Name Features on Venus." Jet Propulsion Laboratory, March 8, 1991. https://www2.jpl.nasa.gov/magellan/pr1353.html.

Maravigna, Carmelo. "Poche parole sulla Memoria di Madama Jeannette Power intorno alle conchiglie fossili nei circonvicini di Milazzo." *l'Innominato*, no. 12 (August 20, 1837): 236–237.

Mitoh, Sayaka, and Yoichi Yusa. "Extreme Autotomy and Whole-Body Regeneration in Photosynthetic Sea Slugs." *Current Biology* 31, no. 5 (2021): R233–R234.

Owen, Richard. "Mollusca." *Encyclopaedia Britannica*, 8th ed. Accessed January 13, 2022. https:// digital.nls.uk/encyclopaedia-britannica/archive/193596964#?c=0&m=0&s=0&cv=341&xywh =2211%2C474%2C3726%2C2765.

"Power Cage." STATE Studio. Accessed September 30, 2020. https://state-studio.com/program /studiorix-98a52-s8lh9-z9gzd.

Rehbock, Philip F. "The Victorian Aquarium in Ecological and Social Perspective." In *Oceanography: The Past.* New York: Springer, 1980.

Rudwick, Martin J. S. *Scenes from Deep Time: Early Pictorial Representations of the Prehistoric World.* Chicago: University of Chicago Press, 1992.

Epilogue

Finn, Julian K., and Mark D. Norman. "The Argonaut Shell: Gas-Mediated Buoyancy Control in a Pelagic Octopus." *Proceedings of the Royal Society B: Biological Sciences* 277, no. 1696 (2010): 2967–2971.

Grove, S. J., and J. K. Finn. "Unusual Strandings of Greater Argonaut *Argonauta argo* in Southeast Tasmania, Autumn 2014." *Malacological Soc. Australasia News* 151, no. 1 (2014): 3–4.

Helm, Rebecca R. Interview with the author, June 4, 2020.

FURTHER READING

Emling, Shelley. *The Fossil Hunter: Dinosaurs, Evolution, and the Woman Whose Discoveries Changed the World*. New York: St. Martin's Griffin, 2011.

Fessenden, Marissa. "A 19th Century Shipwreck Might Be Why This Naturalist Faded to Obscurity." *Smithsonian*, June 2, 2015. https://www.smithsonianmag.com/smart-news/19th-century -shipwreck-might-be-why-famous-female-naturalists-name-faded-obscurity-180955468/.

Lendler, Ian. *The First Dinosaur: How Science Solved the Greatest Mystery on Earth*. New York: Margaret K. McElderry Books, 2019.

Montgomery, Sy. *The Octopus Scientists: Exploring the Mind of a Mollusk*. Boston: Houghton Mifflin Harcourt, 2015.

Newman, Patricia. *Planet Ocean: Why We All Need a Healthy Ocean*. Minneapolis: Millbrook Press, 2021.

Parsons, Eleanor. "The Lady and the Argonauts." *New Scientist* 233, no. 3114 (2017): 40–41.

Scales, Helen. *Spirals in Time: The Secret Life and Curious Afterlife of Seashells*. New York: Bloomsbury Sigma, 2016.

Sidman, Joyce. *The Girl Who Drew Butterflies: How Maria Merian's Art Changed Science*. New York: Houghton Mifflin Harcourt, 2018.

Swaby, Rachel. *Headstrong: 52 Women Who Changed Science—and the World*. New York: Broadway Books, 2015.

Young, Lauren J. "The Seamstress and the Secrets of the Argonaut Shell." *Science Friday*. Accessed January 13, 2022. https://www.sciencefriday.com/articles/the-seamstress-and-the-secrets-of -the-argonaut-shell/.

Zielinski, Sarah. "Wealth of Cephalopod Research Lost in a 19th Century Shipwreck." *Science News*. Accessed January 13, 2022. https://www.sciencenews.org/blog/wild-things/wealth-cephalopod -research-lost-19th-century-shipwreck.

INDEX

ammonite, 34, 96–97
Anning, Mary, 33–34, 54, 86, 96, 108
Antoinette, Marie, 19
aquariums, 5, 47, 49–50, 53, 55–56, 64, 79, 108, 114
    aquarium craze, 8, 97–99
    invention of, 8–9, 44–46, 57, 88, 95–96, 99, 104–105, 109, 112
    Power cages, 5, 38, 41, 44, 51–52, 54–55, 57, 64–65, 71, 75, 82–83, 99, 102
    public aquariums, 5, 51, 55, 89, 109, 115
argonaut, 5–6, 8–10, 34, 43, 47, 55, 81, 87, 90–91, 96–97, 108–109
    anatomy, 59, 76, 92
    behavior, 59–60, 63–65, 67, 72, 74, 83, 111–113
    evolution, 70, 77
    males, 8, 75–77, 99–100, 113
    naming, 58
    reproduction, 68–71, 83, 85, 113
    shell creation, 63, 67, 69–71, 74, 84–85, 99–100, 111, 113–114
    species, 62–63, 80, 111–112

biographical research, 7, 16, 22, 25–26, 34, 82, 105–107, 115
Blainville, Henri de, 84–85, 90
Bonaparte, Napoleon, 14–16, 18, 20–21, 27, 33, 39, 104–105
butterflies, 30

calcium carbonate, 61, 69, 114
Carcinococcus poweriae, 48

cephalopod, 57, 60–61, 62, 64, 69, 73, 76–77, 96, 99–100, 114
chemise, 6, 19, 108
Cocco, Anastasio, 47, 54, 79, 86, 89, 103
cowrie, 74
Cuvier, Georges, 32–34, 55, 60, 75, 77, 83, 84, 87, 100

diving bell, 46

embalming, 35–36
ethics, 72, 73, 102
experiments, 9, 12, 35–36, 37–38, 42, 46, 49–50, 52–55, 57, 65, 68, 71–72, 74–75, 78, 81, 85, 87–88, 90, 98, 104, 109–111

Fata Morgana, 28–29
fishing industry, 5, 43–44, 47, 63–64, 101–102, 111
fossil, 25, 30, 32–34, 54, 86–88, 95–96, 111
fossil record, 62, 97
France, 12–13, 20, 53, 90, 93, 102, 105–106, 108
    Juillac, 10–11, 17–18, 82, 90, 105–108, 115
    Orléans, 16–18, 106
    Paris, 6, 10–11, 13–14, 16, 18–19, 20–22, 24–25, 32–33, 44, 81, 83–84, 105–106, 108
French Republic, 11–12, 13
French Revolution, 11–13, 15, 18–19, 25, 33, 44, 102
    guillotine, 11, 12, 14, 19, 82
    Louis XVI (king), 11–12, 19–20
    Robespierre, Maximilien, 12

Gonostomus poweriae, 86, 89
Great Britain, 9, 14, 17, 22, 33–34, 86, 88, 90, 96–97
    London, 28, 79, 83, 85, 86, 90, 96–100, 109
Guida per la Sicilia (Villepreux-Power), 90, 108

historian, 5, 9, 52, 57, 82, 105, 107, 115
historical accuracy, 7, 13
hypothesis, 9, 60, 63, 74–75, 79, 88, 99

ichthyosaur, 33–34
Industrial Revolution, 44
Italy, 14, 24–25, 27, 41, 89–90, 102
Itinerario della Sicilia (Villepreux-Power), 90

Kölliker, Albert von, 99

map, 14, 24, 90–91, 107, 109, 112
Maravigna, Carmelo, 79, 81, 83, 85
Maria Carolina di Borbone, 19–21, 25
    wedding dress of, 6, 20–21, 25, 74
marine biology, 9–10, 12, 41–44, 84, 94, 98–99, 102, 108–109, 115
Mediterranean Sea, 5, 40, 42, 45, 55, 58–59, 62
Merian, Maria Sibylla, 30, 54
meteorology, 93, 109
metric system, 12–13
Mignonne, 36–37, 81
mollusk, 10, 49, 55, 57, 60–61, 69–70, 86–87, 99, 111, 113

naturalist, 7, 28, 32, 35, 43, 45, 47, 54, 56–57, 59, 63, 67–69, 74, 79, 84, 98, 110, 115

nautilus, 62–63, 113

Nicot, Jeanne. *See* Villepreux, Jeanne

octopus, 4–6, 8–9, 22, 33–34, 42, 56–57, 61–62, 65, 68–70, 72–73, 75–76, 91, 99–100, 102, 111, 113–114

anatomy, 43, 55, 59–60, 64

See also argonaut

Owen, Caroline, 87–88, 104

Owen, Richard, 86–88, 99

paleontology, 32, 34, 84

Paris, 87

pine marten, 5, 37–40, 44, 63, 72, 81, 91, 108–109, 113

Pliny, 56–57, 59, 63, 74, 111

Poli, Giuseppe Saverio, 68

Power, James, 19, 22, 25–27, 37, 81, 85, 92, 99, 103–106

birthplace of, 21

family of, 21, 82

Rang, Sander, 83–84, 85

Reign of Terror, 12

Riccio, Mariano, 30

scientific society, 8, 34–35, 104

Gioenia Academy, 8, 81

Linnean Society, 80–81, 104

Royal Society of London, 79–80, 86

Zoological Society of London, 83, 90

scuba diving, 46, 66, 94, 111

sea star, 22, 45, 50, 53, 79, 91

sewing, 6, 14, 18, 20, 97

sexism, 8, 26–27, 34, 109

shipwreck, 7, 9, 46, 48, 86, 88, 91, 115

shrimp, barrel, 47–48

Sicily, 5–7, 9, 14, 23–24, 28–31, 40, 42, 59, 65, 73, 82, 85, 88, 90–91, 93, 99, 102, 104, 115

Catania, 81, 83, 91

Ferdinand I (king), 25

Messina, 8, 24–26

Mount Etna, 37, 63

port of Messina, 8, 21, 24, 66, 108

Strait of Messina, 24, 28, 41–42, 51, 86, 89, 103

slavery, 12, 21, 72

snail, 5, 22, 33, 42, 52–53, 60, 61, 73, 84, 91, 101, 113

triton, 53–54, 79

woody canoe-bubble, 49–50, 55

taxonomy, 47

Linnaeus, Carl, 63, 80

Thynne, Anna, 97–98

tortoise, 5, 36–37, 79, 91

United States, 8, 13, 72, 97

Venus, 107–108, 114

Villepreux, Gabrielle, 15

Villepreux, Jeanne, 11–12, 14–15

Villepreux, Joseph, 91

Villepreux, Pierre, 11–12, 14–15, 17, 21, 91

Villepreux-Power, Jeanne

birth of, 12

death of, 105

drawings of, 7, 9, 18, 31, 48, 54, 81, 88, 109

education of, 14–16, 24, 26

husband of (*see* Power, James)

inventions of, 8–9, 35–36 (*see also* aquariums)

marriage of, 22

nicknames of, 14–15

pets of, 27, 35, 39 (*see also* Mignonne; pine marten)

photograph of, 7, 91–92

research of (*see* argonaut; butterflies; experiments; marine biology; meteorology; snail)

writings of, 5, 7, 9, 10, 17, 23–24, 28, 29–31, 35–38, 41, 43–44, 47–48, 54, 57–58, 63, 65, 67–70, 72, 74–75, 83, 90–91, 99, 102, 110 (see also *Guida per la Sicilia*; *Itinerario della Sicilia*)

Villepreux-Power Patera, 107–108, 114

Vinciguerria poweriae, 89

war, 14, 16–17, 25, 81, 100, 104–105, 106

waterspout, 29, 93

PHOTO ACKNOWLEDGMENTS

Image credits: Gerald Robert Fischer/Shutterstock, p. 4; Shpatak/Shutterstock, p. 6; The Picture Art Collection/Alamy Stock Photo, pp. 7, 85; DEA/A. DAGLI ORTI/Getty Images, p. 8; Hemis/Alamy Stock Photo, p. 11; ZU_09/DigitalVision/Getty Images, pp. 12, 101; Harvard Art Museums/Wikimedia Commons (public domain), p. 15; PRISMA ARCHIVO/Alamy Stock Photo, p. 17; Timken Collection, National Gallery of Art, Washington DC, p. 19; DEA PICTURE LIBRARY/De Agostini/Getty Images, p. 20; Marzolino/Shutterstock, p. 25; DEA /V. PIROZZI/De Agostini/Getty Images, p. 26; Wellcome Collection, pp. 28, 45, 73, 86, 99; Rijksmuseum, Amsterdam, p. 29; Biodiversity Heritage Library/flickr, p. 30; Wellcome Library, London/Wikimedia Commons, p. 32; Natural History Museum, London/Wikimedia Commons (public domain), p. 34 (left); © Natural History Museum, London/Bridgeman Images, p. 34 (right); Lubos Houska/Shutterstock, p. 36; Matt_Gibson/iStock/Getty Images, p. 39; damnederangel/iStock/Getty Images, p. 42; Internet Archive Book Images/flickr, pp. 43, 81; Classic Image/Alamy Stock Photo, p. 46; BIOSPHOTO/Alamy Stock Photo, pp. 48, 71; agefotostock/Alamy Stock Photo, p. 49; © RMN-Grand Palais/Art Resource, NY, pp. 51, 92, 104; Dkontogiannnis/Wikimedia Commons (CC BY-SA 3.0), p. 53; Albert Kok/Wikimedia Commons (public domain), p. 55; University of Toronto Wenceslaus Hollar Digital Collection/Wikimedia Commons (public domain), p. 56; PhotoStock-Israel/Alamy Stock Photo, p. 59; Ed Reschke/Photodisc/Getty Images, p. 61 (top left); Sahara Frost/Shutterstock, p. 61 (top right); Bence Sibalin/Shutterstock, p. 61 (middle left); mariusz.ks/Shutterstock, p. 61 (middle right); Martin Strmiska/Alamy Stock Photo, p. 61 (bottom left); Reinhard Dirscherl/The Image Bank/Getty Images, p. 61 (bottom right); by wildestanimal/Moment/Getty Images, p. 62; Fine Art Photographic/Stone/Getty Images, p. 64; National Portrait Gallery, Smithsonian Institution; gift of the Morris and Gwendolyn Cafritz Foundation, p. 66; DEA/G. CIGOLINI/De Agostini/Getty Images, p. 67; Blue Planet Archive/Alamy Stock Photo, pp. 69, 110; Brook Peterson/Stocktrek Images/Getty Images, p. 70; NIH/National Library of Medicine/Wikimedia Commons, p. 72; Gavin Parsons/Alamy Stock Photo, p. 74; 19th era 2/Alamy Stock Photo, p. 75; Wikimedia Commons (public domain), pp. 79, 80, 100; Courtesy Claude Arnal/Association Jeanne Villepreux-Power, p. 82; Library Book Collection/Alamy Stock Photo, p. 84 (top); luca85/Shutterstock, p. 84 (bottom); Dante Fenolio/Science Source, p. 89; British Library/flickr, pp. 90, 91; National Museum Cardiff/Wikimedia Commons (public domain), p. 95; Tiia Monto/Wikimedia Commons (CC BY-SA 3.0), p. 96; Chronicle/Alamy Stock Photo, p. 98; Old Books Images/Alamy Stock Photo, p. 103; Courtesy Anne-LAN, pp. 105, 108; NASA/JPL, p. 107; BIOSPHOTO/Alamy Stock Photo, p. 113; © Simon Grove, p. 115.

Front cover: Gerald Robert Fischer/Shutterstock.com. Back cover: The Picture Art Collection/Alamy Stock Photo. Design elements: Vasya Kobelev/Shutterstock.com.